4ᵗʰ June 2001
Lawrence, KS

Qualitative Inquiry

Qualitative Inquiry

A Dictionary of Terms

Thomas A. Schwandt

SAGE Publications
International Educational and Professional Publisher
Thousand Oaks   London   New Delhi

For information address:

SAGE Publications, Inc.
2455 Teller Road
Thousand Oaks, California 91320
E-mail: order@sagepub.com

SAGE Publications Ltd.
6 Bonhill Street
London EC2A 4PU
United Kingdom

SAGE Publications India Pvt. Ltd.
M-32 Market
Greater Kailash I
New Delhi 110 048 India

Printed in the United States of America

Library of Congress Cataloging-in-Publication Data

Schwandt, Thomas A.
    Qualitative inquiry: A dictionary of terms/author, Thomas A. Schwandt
    p. cm.
    Includes bibliographical references.
    ISBN 0-7619-0253-8 (acid-free paper).—ISBN 0-7619-0254-6
  (pbk.: acid-free paper)
    1. Social sciences—Methodology—Dictionaries.
    2. Social sciences—Research—Dictionaries. I. Title.
H61.S4435 1997   97-4587
300'.72—dc21

            00 01 02 03 10 9 8 7 6 5 4

Acquiring Editor: Peter Labella
Editorial Assistant: Frances Borghi
Production Editor: Sanford Robinson
Production Assistant: Karen Wiley
Typesetter/Designer: Marion S. Warren
Cover Designer: Candice Harman
Print Buyer: Anna Chin

■ Contents

We accept the fact that the subject presents itself historically under different aspects at different times or from a different standpoint. We accept that these aspects do not simply cancel one another out as research proceeds, but are like mutually exclusive conditions that exist each by themselves and combine only in us. Our historical consciousness is always filled with a variety of voices in which the echo of the past is to be heard. It is present in the multifariousness of such voices: this constitutes the nature of the tradition in which we want to share and have a part.

H.-G. Gadamer, 1990

■ Preface

This book is a collection of selected words in a specific research language and their definitions. The language in question is the set of terms and phrases that partially shape the nature, purpose, logic, meaning, and methods of the practices called qualitative inquiry. A guide to the vocabulary of the practices collectively spoken of as qualitative inquiry can be particularly useful because the vocabulary is given different interpretations in the various theoretical perspectives and philosophies of social inquiry—for example: naturalism, feminist theory, symbolic interactionism, phenomenological sociology, philosophical hermeneutics, critical theory, postmodernism—that shape the activity of qualitative inquiry.

The *Dictionary* is intended as a reference book for this vocabulary; it is more like a lexicon than a dictionary in the strict sense of the term. It does not include all the words in the language of qualitative work nor does it claim to display essential definitions of terms and phrases. The choice of entries and the construction of their definitions reflect my particular understanding of various concepts and issues that help define the field. I have tried to make the definitions of entries inviting, inclusive of multiple and often contested points of view, and occasionally provocative. My aim has been to write definitions in such a way that discussion of concepts and issues is stimulated and not foreclosed.

I selected entries on the basis of several considerations. I included terms that graduate students frequently asked about in qualitative methods courses; terms that are constitutive of the methodologies of qualitative inquiry as evident in extended discussion in the literature; and terms that are generally poorly understood or often misused. There are fewer terms dealing with the technical aspects of methods and procedures than with philosophical and methodological concepts because the former are very well covered in the qualitative methods literature in all fields.

My own prejudices about what makes for sound social inquiry also guided selection of terms. This book has its origins in my experiences with teaching courses in social and educational research in general and in qualitative inquiry in particular. In the past decade, there has been a rapid expansion in the academy, particularly in the professional schools, of so-called qualitative methods courses. Opinions vary on just how such a course should be composed. For several years, I (and recently two other colleagues) have been teaching separate sections of a semester-long doctoral course in qualitative methods principally to students in various fields of education but also including students studying business, telecommunications, journalism, linguistics, anthropology, leisure studies, counseling, nursing, and library science. A few years ago, we were able to develop a second course devoted exclusively to foundational issues. We have also managed to add advanced seminars on various aspects of qualitative methodology, but the qualitative methods course continues to be *the* single course required or strongly recommended in many programs of study. Hence, there is a great deal of pressure on the course to cover methods for generating and analyzing data, fieldwork procedures and logistics, and field relations, as well as foundational issues. The penchant for teaching only social scientific research methods in professional fields that draw on social science disciplines coupled with the general antipathy toward philosophical reflection tends to result in shortchanging foundational issues. Even given the best of intentions, instructors working within the limited time frame of a one-semester course are likely to give short shrift to philosophical matters. Yet, to ignore these issues or to treat them in a cavalier way as the province of only philosophers of social science is intellectually irresponsible on at least two counts. First, with the exception of naturalism, the intellectual traditions that inform qualitative methodologies arise in opposition to the preoccupation with scientific method and all it entails. Thus, an understanding of the various critiques of method foregrounds the definition of the aim and nature of the practical undertaking of qualitative work. Second, ignoring philosophical issues is bad practice from a pedagogical point of view. Invariably, even in a course devoted exclusively to fieldwork procedures and methods, students raise important questions about foundational issues in epistemology and methodology, not only as they relate to qualitative approaches to inquiry but as they define social science inquiry in general. This *Dictionary* is a small attempt to address this concern. By providing an inviting overview of critical terms in the discourses of qualitative inquiry, I aim to avoid both a kind of intellectual and conceptual imperialism that elevates philosophical concerns above all others and at the same time steer clear of a superficial involvement with philosophical labels for critical ideas.

Obviously every term included in this *Dictionary* is discussed with greater depth, breadth, and subtlety in a many other resources. For example, the *Cambridge Dictionary of Philosophy* (Cambridge University Press, 1995) provides extensive definitions of some of the philosophical terms included here, and the 600-plus page *Handbook of Qualitative Research* (Sage, 1994) is a comprehensive examination of many issues comprising the philosophies and methodologies of qualitative work. It was not my intention to offer a detailed, nuanced treatment of each entry. The more modest goal of this book is to provide an adequate introduction to the terms that help constitute the practices of qualitative inquiry. In this way, the book serves as a guidebook. This guide is both descriptive and normative. It is both *about* the vocabulary constitutive of the practices of qualitative inquiry and, in many instances, also *evaluative of* that vocabulary. I make no attempt to conceal my efforts to engage in a critical evaluation of many of the concepts discussed here, and the Introduction reveals more about my predispositions.

To encourage readers to undertake further examination of issues, I opted to include references in most of the entries. The selection of references was guided by a pedagogical interest in helping acquaint readers with the complexity of the issues that shape the various understandings of qualitative inquiry without sending them to numerous additional or not readily accessible references. Whenever prudent I used the same reference for more than one entry. Bibliographic information for references is provided in each entry. This makes for some redundancy but it facilitates ready access to the references. A list of the primary references is provided at the end of the book. Branching from the bibliographies provided in the sources cited here will quickly lead to additional resources for the interested reader.

This *Dictionary* can be used in a variety of ways. Used in conjunction with a few texts representative of different theoretical perspectives on qualitative inquiry, the *Dictionary* can be one of the primary texts in a course in the logic or foundations of qualitative or interpretive inquiry. Students can use the *Dictionary* as a starting pointing to launch their own investigations into various topics that they then present to members of the class. It can be used as a supplementary text in a course that seeks to cover something of both the foundations and the methods of qualitative inquiry. Students could work individually or in small groups with clusters of related terms to explore interrelationships (e.g., Emic/Etic, Participant Observation, Fieldwork, Ethnographic Naturalism; or Ethnographic Realism, Crisis of Representation, Text, Voice; or Objective/Objectivity, Subjective/Subjectivity, Objectivism, Subjectivism, Realism, Skepticism; or Method, Bias, Coding, Computer-Assisted Data Analysis, Fieldnotes; or Criteria, Problem of Criteria, Reliability, Validity, Triangulation, Trustworthiness Criteria, Authenticity Criteria; or Critical Social Science, Theory, Explanation, *Verstehen*, Naturalism, Antinaturalism, Pluralism). Any number of combinations of terms are possible for this kind of exploration. The *Dictionary* may also be used simply as a supplementary resource for lectures in general methods courses. Students can find an initial understanding of a term in the *Dictionary* and then be encouraged to pursue more thorough exploration of the concept on their own, with fellow students, or in conversations with the instructor. I look forward to hearing from readers about their experiences with the *Dictionary*.

I owe a great debt to my graduate students over the past 10 years whose questions about the ideas that I try to explain in this book always serve to teach me and inspire me to learn more. For her support, encouragement, willingness to listen, and invitations to further reflection, I thank my best friend, colleague, and companion, Colleen Larson. Conversations over the years with colleagues too numerous to mention in education, philosophy, anthropology, law, sociology, religious studies, journalism, and history about the concepts that are displayed here have simply been invaluable. I received constructive criticism on earlier drafts from Peter Magolda, Luise McCarty, David McCarty, and three anonymous reviewers. David Schwandt prepared the figure that appears in the text on page 64. The final version of this book was completed while I was on leave at Nordlandsforskning, a research institute in northern Norway. To my colleagues there in the social welfare research group, many thanks for providing space, time, and stimulating discussions. Despite all the help I have had, all errors of interpretation of issues and concepts are of course my responsibility. I am indebted to Mitch Allen of AltaMira Press, who planted the idea of doing this kind of book, and to Peter Labella of Sage Publications for enthusiastically supporting it. Finally, this book is for you, Sarah.

—Thomas A. Schwandt

■ Acknowledgment

The figure that appears on page 64 is adapted from *Hermeneutics and Education* by Shaun Gallagher; ©1992 State University of New York Press, Albany; reproduced by permission.

■ Introduction

This *Dictionary* is intended to be a contribution to the ongoing effort to understand the aims and methods of the activities collectively called qualitative inquiry. Although I have tried to be ecumenical in my choice of the vocabulary that in part constitutes those activities, there is no denying the fact that the text is written from my particular point of view about the meaning of the practice of human inquiry in general and of qualitative inquiry in particular. Hence, the following reflections on the preconceptions that shaped (and were in turn reshaped in) the act of writing this *Dictionary* are offered as a framework for understanding the composition of this particular text. These reflections may also serve as a source of ideas for the use of this text. A usual introduction might attempt to spell out the key features of qualitative inquiry. But there are many other sources for the same; hardly a book is published about qualitative study that does not offer some definition of key assumptions, defining characteristics, and so on. What is offered here are some alternative ideas for how we might think about teaching and learning the practice.

Grand Synthesis or Constellation?

Our modernist tendency in surveying the entire scene of the multiple practices of qualitative inquiry is to impose order on the unruly, largely unorganized (and often conflicting) assumptions, features, characteristics, approaches, perspectives, philosophies, methods, and so on that comprise the subject matter of qualitative research methodology. We aim to construct a sense of the subject matter's structure by employing some means of categorizing the various practices by their methodologies, philosophical assumptions, historical lineage, and so on.[1] This tendency has two corollaries: First, it encourages efforts at achieving integration and grand synthesis. This is accomplished by discovering foundational principles, unifying themes, *a* vocabulary of the practice, a definitive set of propositions *about* the practice(s) of qualitative inquiry, or all of these. Second, this approach to knowing the field of qualitative inquiry is detached, uninvolved, and spectatorlike. It is a kind of knowing that requires objectification of that which we seek to understand. It is a knowing from the 'outside.' This general knowledge is expressed as a set of assertions about methodology that apply to different situations, circumstances, and problems under which qualitative inquiry is thought to be most appropriate. These assertions constitute the 'theory' of the practice and they can be explained, investigated, transmitted to novices, contrasted with assertions about other methodological practices, and so forth.[2]

But the study of the practices of qualitative inquiry need not (and perhaps should not) be undertaken in this way. Wittgenstein, among others, has pointed out how words involve a play of different uses and definitions in a "multiplicity of language games."[3] Qualitative inquiry can be thought of as using this analogy. It is a set of multiple practices in which words in methodological and philosophical vocabularies acquire different meanings in their use or in particular acts of speaking about the meaning of the practice. These different ways of speaking form something more like a constellation of contested practices than an integrated, readily surveyable order.[4] There are multiple sources and kinds of disputes, but generally they involve different ways of conceiving of the aim of qualitative inquiry stemming from different traditions of thought.

Rather than gaze on this site of contested practices and its apologists, defenders, critics, and practitioner-disputants from the outside, so to speak, one can engage it by becoming an interlocutor with other practitioners and with 'texts' that form the various traditions of qualitative study. Adopting a posture as partner in the dialogue or conversation about the purpose and means of qualitative inquiry makes possible a different kind of knowing, a knowing from 'within' a particular situation. Here 'knowing' what qualitative inquiry is involves wrestling with what it means *to be* a qualitative practitioner of one sort or another. This kind of knowledge does not take the form of a set of empirically tested propositions, assertions, principles, methods, statements, or ethical codes that define roles and responsibilities that one then adopts to become a so-called qualitative inquirer. The knowledge at issue here is not the general, propositional kind. Rather, it is concerned with understanding specific cases of qualitative inquiry under particular circumstances and dealing with all the complexity, ambiguity, emotions, and volitions entailed in these circumstances. General principles that define qualitative methodologies are not ignored, but they take on meaning only in light of particular cases. The trick is neither to become overwhelmed by the details of particular circumstances nor to be blind to general assumptions, principles, and commitments that define traditions of qualitative study. Rather, one strives to adopt a posture of "perceptive equilibrium"—a dialogue between principles and particulars.[5] In this way, one acquires and exercises practical-moral wisdom of the practice of qualitative inquiry. Simply although somewhat crudely put, one does not 'discover' the orderly reality of either something called the identity or role of the qualitative inquirer or something called the 'principles' of practice of qualitative inquiry; rather one continually constructs and reconstructs that understanding in conversational activities.

The Pedagogical Encounter
With Qualitative 'Texts'

In the act of interpreting a 'text,' whether a written text or conversation with another person, we bring certain fore-conceptions or prejudices that shape our efforts at interpretation. Once we recognize the hermeneutic, dialogical character of the engagement of interpreter and text we become aware of how these fore-conceptions are challenged; how ideas about the meaning of a text are advanced and reshaped in the educative exchange that comprises the encounter. Furthermore, the understanding that results from the encounter is fundamentally a self-understanding, for "interpretation consists of an interchange that involves not only a questioning of subject matter between interpreter and the interpreted, but a self-questioning. The questioning is not just unidirectional or monological; it is reflective or dialogical. All understanding is self-understanding. Interpretation is a questioning of ourselves not only with respect to the subject matter . . . it is also a questioning of ourselves with respect to ourselves and our circumstance."[6] So it was for me in the composition of this *Dictionary.* As I encountered, once again, the vocabulary I have used for many years in talking about the practices of qualitative inquiry, I became aware of how my fore-structure of understanding, my prior knowledge if you will, was being engaged in a critical conversation about the definition and meaning of the practices of qualitative inquiry. My self-understanding—my understanding of self in relation to and application of what I was interpreting—changed.[7] My wish is that students of the aim and methods of qualitative inquiry can experience the same as they encounter this text or others.

The hermeneutic, educative, or pedagogical encounter with qualitative inquiry practices, whether in the interaction with this text or others or in conversations with interpreters and practitioners, can be characterized in terms of several additional principles[8]: (1) Interpretation is both constrained and enabled by traditions and preconceptions. A tradition is not simply some conceptual 'place' from which we come to interpret but also is projected ahead of us in shaping our way of understanding. In the process of interpretation, this tradition itself undergoes rearrangement and transformation. In this sense, the act of learning qualitative inquiry is always 'productive.' (2) The act of interpretation is structured as questioning. Questioning opens both the self-understanding of the interpreter and the meaning of a text to be interpreted to possibilities and restructuring. (3) Interpreting or understanding always involves application. However, "application is meant not in the instrumental or external sense of practicality, but in the more fundamental sense of making something relevant to oneself."[9] The kind of application at stake here is a particular kind of knowledge that was identified earlier as knowing from within, or practical-moral knowledge. Gadamer explains that this is "clearly not objective knowledge—i.e., the knower is not standing over against a situation that he [sic] merely observes; he is directly affected by what he knows. It is something that he has to do." It also differs from technical know-how in that it requires not cleverness in application but understanding: "we discover that the person who is understanding does not know and judge as one who stands apart and unaffected but rather he [sic] thinks along with the other from the perspective of a specific bond of belonging, as if he too were affected."[10]

The Theory-Versus-Practice Divide

Shortly before completing this book, I heard the following anecdote from a colleague at a social research institute in Norway. He had recently attended a conference in health research where presentations were made about the purpose, significance, and meaning of health care. Two different kinds of papers were presented at that conference. Some drew on social and political philosophy to discuss ideas like the phenomenology of care, the place of health institutions in society, and so on. Other papers presented empirical data and the analyses of routine concerns and practices surrounding the daily care of patients (e.g., administering injections, bathing patients). He told me that near the close of the conference he was chatting with another sociologist and asked him what he thought of the presentations. The fellow remarked, "there seemed to be little between Habermas and a bedpan."

This remark is telling for describing various efforts to define and teach social research generally, and qualitative research in particular. Typically, on one hand, we are confronted with texts about the theory of social inquiry. These texts, and the pedagogical circumstances for which they are intended, describe and explain the aim of social theorizing. They draw from various perspectives in twentieth-century Continental philosophy (e.g., critical theory, phenomenology, hermeneutics, structuralism, poststructuralism), Weberian sociology, the blend of American pragmatism and symbolic interactionism, and feminist theory. These texts address the debates about the definition and purpose of social science, the nature of the social world, the question of what constitutes knowledge of that world, the definition of human as opposed to natural sciences, the authority and legitimacy of the social inquirer, and so on. Collectively, this set of material is referred to broadly as the theory or philosophy of qualitative inquiry.

On the other hand, we have texts that carefully describe procedures for generating, analyzing, interpreting, and writing up qualitative data. These texts, and the pedagogical circumstances for which they are intended, focus on the nuts and bolts of fieldwork methods, strategies for framing and interpreting data, and issues of field relations. They serve as instructional aids in the form of either fieldwork guides, handbooks, or personal accounts of fieldwork experience from which we learn about the means of dealing with logistical, procedural, ethical, and political situations. Collectively, this is the stuff referred to as the practice of qualitative work. A common assumption is that this stuff of practice is about everything that theory is not.

Not only is there often little in between these two kinds of approaches to teaching and learning qualitative inquiry, but the effort to sharply distinguish the theory from the practice of qualitative inquiry promotes a false dualism.[11] The continuity of interactions between thinking and doing, between reflection and action, or between technical expertise and the good to be served by what is produced by means of that expertise is evident when we rehabilitate the Aristotelian concept of praxis and apply it to our understanding of the practice of human inquiry.[12]

Praxis is defined not in opposition to theory but in contrast to *poiesis*.[13] The latter is a kind of action directed at the specific end of 'making' or creating a product. The 'end' or goal of *poiesis* can be specified in advance of undertaking the activity. It requires, in turn, a form of reasoning or knowledge called *techne*—technical knowledge or expertise. When the practice of social inquiry is modeled on a trade or craft like carpentry, then the practice is being defined as an activity of *poiesis*.

Praxis also has a goal or end-in-view but that goal is not to produce some product but to realize some morally worthwhile good. As such it requires a form of reasoning called *phronesis* (ethical know-how or practical-moral knowledge). *Phronesis* is characterized by choice, deliberation, and ethical-practical judgment. It is different from technical reasoning in which we simply consider the relative effectiveness of different means to some particular end. When the practice of human inquiry is thought to be analogous to 'doing' ethics and politics, it can be said to be defined as an activity of praxis.

The 'good' to be realized through praxis cannot simply be 'produced' or 'made' by following some specific preestablished procedures or means. The 'goods' of a practice cannot be specified in advance of actually engaging in a practice, nor are these goods fixed and unchangeable. Rather, these goods can be done or accomplished only through simultaneous contemplation of means and ends. Practice is thus "morally committed action."[14]

The end-in-view of praxis at any given time in the history of a practice is intelligible in terms of the practical-moral knowledge comprising the inherited tradition of the practice. To engage in a practice is to be initiated into the theories, concepts, beliefs, understandings, values, indeed the very language that constitutes the practice. A practice is thus laden with theoretical and pretheoretical understandings located in the tradition of the practice. A practitioner simultaneously acknowledges the authority of that tradition and subjects it to criticism. In other words, the "tradition is not mechanically or passively reproduced: It is constantly being reinterpreted and revised through dialogue and discussion about how to pursue the practical goods which constitute the tradition."[15] Acting and thinking, practice and theory are thus linked in a continuous process of self-examination and self-transformation.

Conceived in this way, the practice of social inquiry cannot be adequately defined as an atheoretical 'making' that requires only technical expertise or know-how. For social inquiry is not *poiesis*, a form of activity that does not itself change its own ends through reflection on those ends. Rather, social inquiry is a distinctive praxis, a form of reflective action that itself transforms the theory that guides it. Hence, to divorce the study of the nature and aim of social theorizing; the definition of the human sciences; the study of the ways of knowing; the epistemological relationship of subject-object; the philosophies of structuralism, poststructuralism, phenomenology, and so on from the 'practical' activities of generating and interpreting data in social inquiry is to confuse the very concept of what it means to 'practice' social inquiry.

On Framing Qualitative Studies

The practice of social inquiry in the modern Western tradition is historically modeled as a 'scientific' practice. The activity of social inquiry is thought to be sciencelike, which means its aim is both to pursue and to use scientific theory and to employ 'theoretical' reasoning. For example, many qualitative or 'interpretive' studies stemming from symbolic interactionist, phenomenological, ethnomethodological, and *Verstehen* perspectives employ a 'social scientific' frame: a way of collecting and interpreting qualitative data that places a premium on the validity, relevance, and importance of both topic and findings.[16] The frame is oriented to asking questions about the type, frequency, magnitude, structure, process, causes, consequences, and meanings of sociopolitical phenomena and developing answers to those questions. In this frame, the inquirer faces a problematic situation calling for a solution. Answers or 'solutions' take the form of substantive or middle-range theory explaining or accounting for sociopolitical phenomena. These solutions are 'theoretical' because they have the characteristics of being atemporal or universal (i.e., held to be true across a variety of specific cases) and necessary (i.e., not accidental).[17] A researcher makes sense of the individual case in light of universal principles. In the professional fields, the social scientific enterprise serves the decision-making needs of teachers, social service workers, managers, administrators, health care providers, and so on by providing them with this general knowledge of definitions, principles, and theoretical ideas that these practitioners can then, in turn, apply to solve specific problems.

Apologists for the less well understood hermeneutic tradition that is also a part of the historical narrative of social inquiry, however, challenge this 'scientific' framing of human inquiry. In the hermeneutic tradition, both the practice of social inquiry as well as the practices of teaching, administering, caring, and so forth served by social inquiry are framed as dialogical, interpretive encounters. Neither the social inquirer nor the practitioner is thought to face a problem to be solved as much as a dilemma or mystery that requires interpretation and self-understanding (see foregoing text). The distinction between the two can be illustrated as follows: "A problem is something that can be totally objectified and resolved in objective terms because the person confronting the problem can completely detach himself from it and view it externally. . . . A mystery is something that involves the person in such a way that the person cannot step outside of it to see it in an objective manner. She is caught within the situation with no possibility of escape, and no possibility of clear-cut solutions. Indeed, ambiguity is the rule within a mystery."[18] Furthermore, to understand a 'mystery' is to deal with actual, concrete events and people, in specific places and times under particular circumstances. Universal principles become understandable only in light of specific cases. The kind of reasoning required here involves judgment, deliberation, and the assembly of a variety of empirical, ethical, and political considerations necessary to cope with or make sense of the situation. The 'understanding' that comes from this kind of reasoning has a unique quality:

> Understanding, like action, always remains a risk and never leaves room for the simple application of a general knowledge of rules to the statements or texts to be understood. Furthermore, where it is successful, understanding means a growth in inner awareness, which as a new experience enters into the texture of our own mental experience. Understanding is an adventure, and like any other adventure is dangerous. . . . It affords unique opportunities as well. It is capable of contributing in a special way to the broadening of our human experiences, our self-knowledge, and our horizon, for everything understanding mediates is mediated along with ourselves.[19]

One of the most difficult concepts to grasp about the philosophy of qualitative inquiry is this hermeneutic reframing that entails a radically different way of thinking about what it means to be a social inquirer, a radically different form of reasoning and a radically different kind of knowledge. In this reframing, social inquiry (including qualitative inquiry) is less a 'science' (as construed in the Western tradition of method, mathematics, measurement, and theoretical reasoning) and more a kind of practical philosophy.[20] Understanding the notion that qualitative inquiry is actually a contested site of multiple practices, depends in large part on grasping something of this hermeneutic reframing. Hermeneutics in social inquiry arises in the first instance as a form of opposition to the dominance of logical positivist and logical empiricist perspectives in the human sciences: It is the source of defining interpretation as a genuine alternative to explanation. In the second instance, it is on the 'field of hermeneutics' that contemporary controversies unfold among

xxii QUALITATIVE INQUIRY

apologists for philosophical, critical, and deconstructivist perspectives over adequate accounts of the right aim and meaning of interpretation.

Notes

1. John Shotter (*Conversational Realities*, Sage, 1993, p. 57) describes this as the "modernist way of theory." The distinction between 'knowing from the outside' and 'knowing from within' is based in part on Shotter's discussion of an alternative to this modernist way.

2. The contrast between this kind of conceptual, purely cognitive knowledge and practical wisdom (discussed later) is explained in Jos. P. A. M. Kessels and Fred A. J. Korthagen, "The Relationship Between Theory and Practice: Back to the Classics," *Educational Researcher*, 1996 (2), p. 18; see also Shirley Pendlebury, "Reason and Story in Wise Practice," in *Narrative in Teaching, Learning, and Research*, edited by Hunter McEwan and Kieran Egan (New York: Teachers College Press, 1995), pp. 50-65.

3. Ludwig Wittgenstein, *Philosophical Investigations* (New York: Macmillan, 1968), p. 23.

4. Richard Bernstein borrows from T. Adorno to define a constellation as a "juxtaposed rather than integrated cluster of changing elements that resist reduction to a common denominator, essential core, or generative first principle," *The New Constellation: The Ethical-Political Horizons of Modernity/Postmodernity* (Cambridge, MA: MIT Press, 1991), p. 8.

5. Pendlebury, "Reason and Story in Wise Practice," p. 55.

6. Shaun Gallagher, *Hermeneutics and Education* (Albany: State University of New York Press, 1992), p. 157.

7. Both Gadamer and Ricouer emphasize that hermeneutical self-understanding is not to be equated with the modernist notion of the interpreter's (subject's) reflective discovery of self-consciousness. See Gallagher, *Hermeneutics and Education*, p. 158.

8. These characteristics are drawn from Gallagher, *Hermeneutics and Education*, pp. 188-191, 348-351.

9. Ibid., p. 190.

10. H.-G. Gadamer, *Truth and Method* as quoted in Gallagher, *Hermeneutics and Education*, p. 153.

11. What is claimed here for qualitative inquiry holds true for all of social science inquiry more generally.

12. For views of hermeneutics as practical philosophy see, for example, Hans-Georg Gadamer, *Reason in the Age of Science* (trans. F. G. Lawrence, Cambridge, MA: MIT Press, 1981); Charles Taylor, *Philosophical Papers*, Vol. 2 (Cambridge, England: Cambridge University Press, 1985).

13. The following discussion is based on Wilfred Carr's explication of praxis. See his *For Education* (Buckingham, England: Open University Press, 1995), pp. 68ff.

14. Ibid., p. 68.

15. Ibid., p. 69.

16. See the discussion of this frame in John Lofland and Lyn H. Lofland, *Analyzing Social Settings* (3rd ed.) (Belmont, CA: Wadsworth, 1995), pp. 149ff.

17. See the discussion of theoretical versus practical reasoning in Albert R. Jonsen and Stephen Toulmin, *The Abuse of Casuistry* (Berkeley: University of California Press, 1988), pp. 23-46.

18. Gallagher, *Hermeneutics and Education*, p. 152.

19. Gadamer, *Reason in the Age of Science*, pp. 110-111.

20. For two examples of what this might look like see, in education, Hunter McEwan, "Narrative Understanding in the Study of Teaching," in *Narrative in Teaching, Learning, and Research* edited by Hunter McEwan and Kieran Egan (New York: Teachers College Press, 1995), pp. 166-183; in management, John Shotter's discussion of "The Manager as Practical Author: Conversations for Action," in his *Conversational Realities* (Newbury Park, CA: Sage, 1993), pp. 148-159.

■ Conventions

Terms are listed alphabetically without regard to hyphens and spaces between words.

- Cross-references are given at the end of each entry and signaled by the bold-faced designation **See also.**
- *Italics* are used for foreign words and phrases, and titles of books and journals.
- Single quotes are used to indicate a novel use of a word or phrase.
- <u>Underlining</u> is used on rare occasions to mark off sections within a long entry and for emphasis.
- Some entries contain terms or phrases discussed elsewhere in the *Dictionary*. When explanation of another term would be helpful for understanding a particular entry, the term in question appears in ***bold-faced italics***.

ACTION RESEARCH The term was coined by social psychologist Kurt Lewin (1890-1947) in the 1940s to describe a particular kind of research that united the experimental approach of social science with programs of social action to address social problems. Lewin argued that social problems (as opposed to a scientist's own theoretical interests) should serve as the impulse for social research. He developed a model of social inquiry that involved a spiral of interlocking cycles of planning, acting, observing, and reflecting. Although Lewin's approach was well received in organizational research in the 1960s and 1970s, it was subject to various criticisms within the social scientific community, that is, that it was not really 'research' because it did not meet criteria of a valid 'scientific' methodology; that it was little more than refined common sense and not rigorous empirical research; that it blurred an important distinction that should be maintained between theory and practice. Various forms of action

A

research are alive and well today, however, in the fields of education, organizational and socioeconomic development, and work life. These research approaches are often identified by different labels—for example: action inquiry, action science, participatory inquiry, collaborative inquiry, cooperative inquiry, participatory action research—that mark distinctions from Lewin's original formulation.

Building on the work of both Lewin and John Dewey (1859-1952), Chris Argyris and Donald Schön developed a particular form of action research called action science. It seeks to advance basic (or theoretical) knowledge while it simultaneously aims to solve practical problems in organizations and communities. It provides strategies for both problem framing or setting and problem solving and links the two activities in a feedback cycle called "double loop learning." Action scientists "engage with participants in a collaborative process of critical inquiry into problems of social practice in a learning context" (C. Argyris, R. Putnam, and D. M. Smith, *Action Science*, Jossey-Bass, 1985, p. 237) in which reflection and experimentation are ongoing (see also Donald Schön, *The Reflective Practitioner: How Professionals Think in Action*, Basic Books, 1983). Action science employs a variety of methods for generating data including observations, interviews, action experiments, and participant-written cases and accounts. A variation of Argyris and Schön's approach called 'action inquiry' has been developed by the organizational theorist William Torbert (*The Power of Balance: Transforming Self, Society, and Scientific Inquiry*, Sage, 1991).

According to Wilfred Carr and Stephen Kemmis (*Becoming Critical*, Falmer Press, 1986) all action research has the aims of improvement and involvement: Involvement refers to the participation of practitioners in all phases of planning, acting, observing, and reflecting; improvement in the situation in which a particular social practice takes place, the understanding practitioners have of their practice, the practice itself, or all of these. **See also PARTICIPATORY ACTION RESEARCH.**

ANALYTIC GENERALIZATION   This is a type of generalizing in which the inquirer links findings from a particular *case* to a *theory*. (Here theory means something more like a set of theoretical tools, models, or concepts rather than a formalized set of propositions,

A

laws, and generalizations comprising a systematic, unified, causal explanation of social phenomena.) Also called "theoretical elaboration," this process is what makes it possible for the interpretive anthropologist Clifford Geertz to say that the ethnographer makes small facts speak to large issues (see "Thick Description: Toward an Interpretive Theory of Culture," in Geertz, *The Interpretation of Cultures*, Basic Books, 1973). A study of some phenomenon in a particular set of circumstances (i.e., a 'case') is used as evidence to support, contest, refine, or elaborate a theory, model, or concept (note that the case is never regarded as a definitive test of the theory). For a fuller explanation see D. Vaughan, "Theory Elaboration: The Heuristics of Case Analysis" in C. C. Ragin and H. S. Becker, eds., *What Is a Case?: Exploring the Foundations of Social Inquiry*, Cambridge Univ. Press, 1992.

Many researchers argue that qualitative studies of cases or instances of phenomena are generalizable to concepts, theoretical propositions, or models and not to universes or populations of cases or instances. Hence, analytic generalization is contrasted with statistical generalization. In statistical generalization a case is a sample drawn from a population of cases. An inference is then made about the population based on the study of the characteristics of the sample. On this distinction see R. Yin, *Case Study Research*, 2nd ed., Sage, 1994. **See also CASE STUDY RESEARCH, GENERALIZATION.**

ANALYTIC INDUCTION   A strategy for analyzing qualitative data based on the assumption that the inquirer should formulate propositions that apply to all instances (or cases) of the problem under analysis. After initial examination of the data, the inquirer develops working hypotheses to explain the data. One example, instance, episode, or case in the data corpus is examined to determine whether the hypothesis fits the facts of that instance. If the hypothesis fits, the inquirer moves to the next instance and again tests for fit. If the hypothesis does not fit the facts, the hypothesis is revised or the phenomenon to be explained is redefined to exclude that instance. Instances that do not fit the hypothesis are called negative instances or cases. The intent here is to use negative instances for continuous refinement of the hypothesis until all instances can be satisfactorily explained. For a fuller explanation of the method and a critique see

A

N. Denzin, *The Research Act,* 3rd ed., Prentice Hall, 1989. **See also** ANALYZING QUALITATIVE DATA.

ANALYZING QUALITATIVE DATA   Broadly conceived, this is the activity of making sense of, interpreting, or theorizing the data. It is both art and science, and it is undertaken by means of a variety of procedures that facilitate working back and forth between data and ideas. It includes the processes of organizing, reducing, and describing the data; drawing conclusions or interpretations from the data, and warranting those interpretations. If data could speak for themselves, analysis would not be necessary.

Some qualitative inquirers place a premium on analysis as a science and stress the fact that analysis should be rigorous, disciplined, systematic, carefully documented, and methodical. A good example of this definition of analysis is found in M. Miles and A. M. Huberman, *Qualitative Data Analysis: An Expanded Sourcebook,* 2nd ed., Sage, 1994. This emphasis is also evident in the approach to data analysis adopted by some ethnomethodologists and in approaches to analysis that rely on computer-assisted means. In discussing the ways in which inquirers make sense of their data, Harry Wolcott (*Transforming Qualitative Data,* Sage, 1994) reserves the term "analysis" for these systematic approaches to dealing with qualitative data. He contrasts analysis with description and interpretation: Description answers the question "What's going on here?"; analysis is concerned with the systematic identification of essential features (themes, concepts, assertions) and their interrelationships; interpretation addresses questions like "How does it all mean?" and "What is to be made of it all?"

From a standard social scientific frame of reference using the term "analysis" in its broadest sense, we can make these general observations about the activity: Analysis in qualitative inquiry is recursive and begins almost at the outset of generating data. The inquirer employs a variety of analytic strategies that involve sorting, organizing, and reducing the data to something manageable and then exploring ways to reassemble the data to interpret them. Sorting and organizing requires comparing, contrasting, and labeling the data. This initial step is necessary to bring some order to the largely undifferentiated mass of data that the inquirer has generated from observations, interviews, and so on. Sorting can involve making frequency counts of the data, developing categories or typologies to account for all the data, selecting concepts that define relationships among categories, formulating working hypotheses or assertions that explain the data, or all of these. The results of data analysis can be presented in tables, graphs, charts, concept maps, and narrative accounts. For a thorough examination of dimensions and strategies of analysis conceived in this way, see M. D. LeCompte and J. Preissle, *Ethnography and Qualitative Design in Educational Research*, 2nd ed., Academic Press, 1993; J. Lofland and L. H. Lofland, *Analyzing Social Settings*, 3rd ed., Wadsworth, 1995.

This traditional understanding of analyzing qualitative data is based on a model of scientific analysis most evident in chemistry and physics. To analyze means to break down a whole into its component or constituent parts. Through reassembly of the parts one comes to understand the integrity of the whole. Thus, the qualitative analyst breaks down the whole corpus of data (fieldnotes, transcriptions, and the like) by categorizing and coding its segments and then tries to establish a pattern for the whole by relating the codes or categories to one another. In this way of thinking about analysis, emphasis is placed on knowledge of particular procedures, a 'knowing-how' (e.g., constant comparison method, typological analysis, grounded theory analysis). Notwithstanding the fact that knowledge of particular procedures may be useful in learning what it means to analyze qualitative data, this conception of analysis grounded in scientific *behaviorism* or functionalism is not the only way to conceive of the activity of analysis. For example, hermeneutics models 'analysis' on a dialogue between the analyst (interpreter) and the 'object' of analysis (in this case the data in the form of various texts like fieldnotes, transcriptions, and so on). A deconstructionist approach to analysis views the activity as playing or dancing. **See also COD-ING, COMPUTER-ASSISTED DATA ANALYSIS, DECONSTRUCTIONISM, HERMENEUTIC CIRCLE.**

ANTINATURALISM   One of four basic approaches to the study of social phenomena (the others are naturalism, pluralism, and critical social science). Antinaturalists claim that the study of social phenomena cannot/should not be undertaken using the same methods of inquiry and with the same goal and modes of explanation that the natural sciences employ to study natural phenomena. For the anti-naturalist, there are particular and distinctive features of the social world that make it impossible to do so: (1) The social or human sciences deal with the subject matter of *human action* (vs. the behavior of physical phenomena) and, therefore, (2) the inquirer must attempt to understand (vs. explain) this action by reference to the ways in which humans experience their activities and give meanings to them. Antinaturalists include those who embrace *Verstehen* approaches, *phenomenological sociology,* and *philosophical hermeneutics* as well as some feminist inquirers. **See also** CRITICAL SOCIAL SCIENCE, EXPLANATION, NATURALISM, PLURALISM.

AUDITING   A procedure whereby a third-party examiner systematically reviews the audit trail maintained by the inquirer. The purpose of the audit is to render a judgment about the dependability of procedures employed by the inquirer and the extent to which the conclusions or findings of the study are confirmable. This procedure was first explained by Yvonna Lincoln and Egon Guba in *Naturalistic Inquiry,* Sage, 1985; it was extensively discussed in Thomas Schwandt and Edward Halpern, *Linking Auditing and Metaevaluation,* Sage, 1989. **See also** AUDIT TRAIL, TRUSTWORTHINESS CRITERIA.

AUDIT TRAIL   An organized collection of materials that includes the data generated in a study; a statement of the theoretical framework that shaped the study at the outset; explanations of concepts, models, and the like that were developed as part of the effort to make sense of the data (often the product of *memoing*); a description of the procedures used to generate data and analyze them; a statement of the findings or conclusions of the investigation; notes about the process of conducting the study; personal notes; and copies of instruments used to guide the generation and analysis of data. An audit trail is a systematically maintained documentation system. It can serve dual purposes: It can be used by the inquirer as a means of managing recordkeeping and encouraging reflexivity about procedures, and it can be used by a third-party examiner to attest to the use of dependable procedures and the generation of confirmable findings on the part of the inquirer. **See also** AUDITING, TRUSTWORTHINESS CRITERIA.

AUTHENTICITY CRITERIA   A set of criteria (and associated procedures) developed by Yvonna Lincoln and Egon Guba in *Fourth
Generation Evaluation* (Sage, 1989) for judging the kind of qualitative
inquiry that has its origins in a constructivist epistemology. The criteria are: (1) Fairness—refers to the extent to which the respondents'
different constructions and their underlying values are solicited and
represented in a balanced, even-handed way by the inquirer. ('Constructions' are defined by Lincoln and Guba as the outcomes of
various ways that individuals have of making sense of some situation, event, and so on.) (2) Ontological authenticity—concerned
with the extent to which respondents' own constructions are enhanced or made more informed and sophisticated as a result of their
having participated in the inquiry. (3) Educative authenticity—concerned with the extent to which participants in an inquiry develop
greater understanding and appreciation of the constructions of others. (4) Catalytic authenticity—refers to the extent to which action is
stimulated and facilitated by the inquiry process. (5) Tactical authenticity—refers to the extent to which participants in the inquiry are
empowered to act. **See also CONSTRUCTIVISM, CRITERIA, PROBLEM
OF CRITERIA, TRUSTWORTHINESS CRITERIA.**

BEHAVIORISM   This is a sociopsychological theory emphasizing determinable and invariant principles of human conduct and social behavior. It is strongly deterministic: Behaviors are associated in lawlike ways with environmental stimuli and reinforcements. It is also reductionistic in that it holds there is no need to invent complex mental constructs to explain why behavior happens. Although the theory is most often associated with behavioral and educational psychology, the doctrine of methodological behaviorism is evident in research traditions in other fields, particularly in political science. Methodological behaviorism is the view that the only truly scientific investigation is that which limits itself to behavioral data, that is, that which can be measured and observed, especially patterns of physical responses to environmental stimuli. **See also HUMAN ACTION.**

BIAS   Perhaps the most common criticism of various forms of qualitative inquiry is that they do not adequately address the problem of bias. Three particular kinds of bias are often cited: (1) bias resulting from overreliance on accessible or *key informants*, selective attention to dramatic events or statements, or both; (2) biasing effects of the presence of the inquirer in the site of investigation; (3) biases stemming from the effects of the respondents and the site on the inquirer. Two senses of the term "bias" are at work in these criticisms. In the first sense, readily found in dictionaries, bias denotes a tendency in inquirers that prevents unprejudiced consideration or judgment. For example, critics argue that the tendency to rely on only certain informants or to cross the line between rapport and friendship in dealing with informants leads to the prejudicial drawing of inferences or generalizing from nontypical or nonrepresentative persons or events. Or the tendency to be unaware of how one's interactions in a field site threaten, disrupt, create, or sustain patterns of social interaction leads to a prejudicial account of social behavior in the site. In the second sense, bias means individual preferences, predispositions, or predilections that prevent neutrality and objectivity. This sense of the term "bias" is evident when an inquirer is criticized for taking the side of or advocating for a particular group of informants (and is thus thought to be incapable of rendering a neutral account of the social interaction); criticized for imposing a priori a theoretical framework or interpretation on the data; or when it appears as though the researcher uses data to confirm a hypothesis, belief, and so forth held before the study was undertaken. Although biases of these kinds are a problem for all methodologies for social investigation, they are thought to be particularly acute in qualitative inquiry because the latter is admittedly an intensely personal experience. *Fieldwork* requires the active, sustained, and long-term involvement of the inquirer with respondents and the cultivation of empathy with and attachment to the people one studies to gain access to their own understandings of their life ways.

It is beyond dispute that sound inquiry practice requires critical reflection on one's actions and predispositions and awareness of the potential both of being deceived and of deceiving one's self. The extent to which bias (as explained here) is believed to be a problem in qualitative studies, however, is related to assumptions about

B

objective *method.* A significant subset of qualitative inquiry is wedded to a conception of method as a device for setting aside or controlling bias. The devotion to method as holding the key to sound inquiry is predicated on the assumption that we need some means of removing our tendencies as everyday human beings to be biased or prejudiced in our investigations of social life so that we may come to have genuine, legitimate, objective knowledge. Since Descartes, at least, social science (and philosophy) has been obsessed with this understanding and pursuit of a strong sense of "Method."

In light of this understanding of method, bias or prejudice is always defined negatively as something that interferes with, prevents or inhibits having true, genuine knowledge. It is precisely this understanding of method and prejudice, however, that is severely criticized by advocates of *philosophical hermeneutics.* For example, Hans-Georg Gadamer's (*Truth and Method,* 2nd ed., Continuum, 1988) critique of the Cartesian notion of method as providing a sure path to knowledge is based in large part on a rehabilitation of the word "prejudice." Building on the work of Martin Heidegger (1889-1976), Gadamer argued that prejudice ('prejudgment') can neither be eliminated nor set aside for it is an inescapable condition of being and knowing. In fact, our understanding of ourselves and our world depends on having prejudgment. What we must do to achieve understanding is to reflect on prejudice (prejudgment) and distinguish enabling from disabling prejudice. **See also** METHOD, OBJECTIVE/OBJECTIVITY, REFLEXIVITY, SUBJECTIVE/SUBJECTIVITY.

BRICOLAGE/BRICOLEUR   These terms have recently been used to characterize the activity of qualitative inquiry. For example, in their introduction to the *Handbook of Qualitative Research* (Sage, 1994, p. 2), editors Norman Denzin and Yvonna Lincoln describe the multiple methodologies used in qualitative inquiry as *bricolage* and the qualitative inquirer as *bricoleur,* one who is "adept at performing a large number of diverse tasks, ranging from interviewing to observing, to interpreting personal and historical documents, to intensive self-reflection and introspection . . . [and one who] reads widely and is knowledgeable about the many interpretive paradigms (feminism, Marxism, cultural studies, constructivism) that can be brought to any particular problem." The term is often traced to Claude Lévi-

Strauss (*The Savage Mind*, Univ. of Chicago Press, 1966, pp. 16-17) who, in seeking to define the savage mind, defined a *bricoleur* as "someone who works with his hands and uses devious means." He sharply contrasted the *bricoleur* and the engineer. The bricoleur draws on a heterogeneous collection of inherited odds and ends kept at hand on the chance they might someday prove useful for some project. What the bricoleur produces is bricolage—a kind of pieced-together (in contrast to algorithmically guided), yet structured solution to a problem. (It should be noted that Jacques Derrida [*Writing and Difference*, trans. A. Bass, Univ. of Chicago Press, 1978, p. 285] criticized this binary distinction, arguing that "if one calls *bricolage* the necessity of borrowing one's concepts from the text of a heritage which is more or less coherent or ruined, it must be said that every discourse is *bricoleur*.")

The special kind(s) of *bricolage* that qualitative inquirers engage in consists of particular configurations of (or ways of relating) various fragments of inherited methodologies, methods, empirical materials, perspectives, understandings, ways of presentation, situated responsiveness, and so on into a coherent, reasoned approach to a research situation and problem. The *bricolage* appears to vary depending on one's allegiance to ideas like hermeneutics, causal explanation, feminist theory, and deconstructionism, to name a few. If there is a theme characterizing much of what passes for qualitative *bricolage*, then it might be resistance to the idea of foundational principles that define the 'true' or 'essential' nature of qualitative epistemology, politics, methodology, and the like (see, for example, the sense of the term *bricolage* employed by Jeffrey Stout, *Ethics After Babel*, Beacon, 1988, pp. 74-75, in his discussion of contemporary problem solving in moral philosophy).

CASE The terms "case" and "unit of analysis" are often used interchangeably in social research, yet to a qualitative inquirer, the term "case" means something more than just "n." In the sociological and anthropological literature a case is typically regarded as a specific and bounded (in time and place) instance of a phenomenon selected for study. The phenomenon of interest may be a person, process, event, group, organization, and so on. Empirical cases are routinely used in the study of law, business, and medicine. Cases are generally characterized on one hand by their concreteness and circumstantial specificity and on the other by their theoretical interest or generalizability. There is disagreement as to whether the case is an empirical unit ('out there' to be discovered and observed) or a theoretical construct that serves the interest of the investigator. The sociologist Howard Becker advises that instead of asking "What is a case?" inquirers should continually ask themselves "What is this a case *of*?"

See C. C. Ragin, "Introduction: Cases of 'What is a case?' " in C. C. Ragin and H. S. Becker, *What Is a Case?: Exploring the Foundations of Social Inquiry*, Cambridge Univ. Press, 1992.

Following a line of reasoning first advanced by Aristotle (*Nichomachean Ethics*, Book VI), some qualitative inquirers argue that knowledge of specific, concrete cases is a different type of knowledge from theoretical or 'scientific' knowledge. The former is a kind of practical wisdom requiring perceptual recognition and the latter a kind of cognitive understanding (or episteme) expressed in rules, principles, theories, and so forth. Yet, in social inquiry the critical issue is how to relate the two kinds of knowledge. On this issue see A. R. Jonsen and S. Toulmin, *The Abuse of Casuistry*, Univ. of California Press, 1988; S. Pendlebury, "Reason and Story in Wise Practice" in H. McEwan and K. Egan, eds., *Narrative in Teaching, Learning, and Research*, Teachers College Press, 1995. **See also** CASE STUDY RESEARCH.

CASE STUDY RESEARCH   This is a strategy for doing social inquiry, although what constitutes the strategy is a matter of some debate. One useful way of thinking of this approach to inquiry is the distinction between case study and variable study: In case study, the case itself is at center stage, not variables (see C. C. Ragin "Introduction: Cases of 'What is a case?' " in C. C. Ragin and H. S. Becker, *What Is a Case?: Exploring the Foundations of Social Inquiry*, Cambridge Univ. Press, 1992). Robert Yin (*Case Study Research: Design and Methods*, rev. ed., Sage, 1989) argues that a case study strategy is preferred when the inquirer seeks answers to how or why questions, when the inquirer has little control over events being studied, when the object of study is a contemporary phenomenon in a real-life context, when boundaries between the phenomenon and the context are not clear, and when it is desirable to use multiple sources of evidence. Robert Stake (*The Art of Case Study Research*, Sage, 1995) emphasizes that the foremost concern of case study research is to generate knowledge of the particular. He explains that case study seeks to discern and pursue understanding of issues intrinsic to the case itself. He acknowledges, however, that cases can be chosen and studied because they are thought to be instrumentally useful in furthering understanding of a particular problem, issue, concept, and so on. Both

Stake and Yin argue that case studies can be used for theoretical elaboration or *analytic generalization*. **See also** CASE, CROSS-CASE ANALYSIS.

CAUSAL ANALYSIS   Causation is intimately related to *explanation*; asking for an explanation of an event is often to ask <u>why</u> it happened. Hence, for many social scientists, deterministic (universal) and statistical (probabilistic) causal laws are thought to play a pivotal role in defining what constitutes a legitimate explanation of social phenomena. Although causal relations are important in social inquiry, exactly how to define a causal relationship is one of the most difficult topics in epistemology and the philosophy of science. There is little general agreement on how to establish causation. Some philosophers and social scientists argue that 'cause' means an underlying *lawlike* mechanism that accounts for the regular observed association of events. Others support an inductive model of causation: A statement of a cause summarizes the regular association of events of type C with events of type E. Still others claim that a cause is best defined as a necessary and sufficient condition for the occurrence of an event (see D. Little, *Varieties of Social Explanation*, Westview Press, 1991).

Experimental designs are generally regarded as the most appropriate means for testing causal inferences. Qualitative inquirers usually do not use such designs, but from that fact we cannot conclude that the study of cause is unimportant in all qualitative work. There are many varieties of qualitative inquiry that aim to develop causal accounts of social phenomena using structural, functional, and materialist explanations as well as causal models using qualitative analogues of statistical explanations. Thus, it is irresponsible and untrue to say that qualitative inquiry as a whole eschews causal analysis (see, for example, J. Lofland and L. H. Lofland, *Analyzing Social Settings*, 3rd ed., Wadsworth, 1995, pp. 136ff.). Some defenders of qualitative work have argued that qualitative inquiry is somehow more attuned to the idea of multiple, probabilistic causes of events than so-called quantitative approaches to the social sciences. But that is not necessarily true either, for quantitative studies in the social sciences rely a great deal on statistical (i.e., probabilistic) explanations involving multiple causes and do not always assume a deterministic view of causality (see, for example, C. C. Ragin, *The Comparative Method: Moving Beyond Qualitative and Quantitative Strategies*, Univ. of California Press, 1987).

To understand the importance (or lack thereof) that causal analysis assumes in qualitative inquiry, we must consider the doctrine of *naturalism*. Defenders of naturalism in social science argue that the goal of social inquiry is to create causal explanations of human behavior (however it may be that cause is defined). Phenomenological and hermeneutic approaches to qualitative inquiry reject causal explanation as the proper goal of the human sciences. They argue that we can only understand or interpret *human action*, that we cannot give a causal explanation of it. Some feminist researchers share in this rejection of naturalism. And postmodern approaches to social inquiry aim to deconstruct all language of cause and effect. **See also** EXPLANATION.

CHICAGO SCHOOL   The Chicago school or tradition of sociology developed in the period from about 1920-1940 in the Department of Social Science and Anthropology at the University of Chicago and is associated with the work of Robert Park (1864-1944), W. I. Thomas (1863-1947), Ernest Burgess (1886-1966), Everett C. Hughes, and their students. It is generally recognized as the primary source of sociological fieldwork. Park introduced the sociology of Georg Simmel (1858-1918) to the sociologists of the Chicago School; other important influences on their work included the pragmatism of G. H. Mead (1863-1931) and John Dewey (1859-1952), the *symbolic interactionism* of Herbert Blumer (1900-1987), and interactions with socioanthropologist colleagues at Chicago. Chicago sociologists practiced a rich variety of ethnographic fieldwork including life histories; community studies; urban ethnographies of 'deviant subcultures' including taxi dancers, hobos, gang members (reflecting Park's advice to students to explore and document the subcultures of the city of Chicago); and studies combining a focus on the nature of work, professional identity, role, and status that developed from the intellectual direction provided by Hughes. The tradition figures prominently not simply in the history of fieldwork but in the professional identity of contemporary sociologists: "Although now well dispersed, the Chicago School still represents a sort of mythical Eden to many contemporary sociologists who locate their personal pedigree and purpose in the profession by tracing back their lineage on the family tree planted in Chicago" (J. VanMaanen, *Tales of the Field*, Univ. of Chicago Press, 1988, p. 20). For a history of the tradition see M. Bulmer, *The Chicago School of Sociology*, Univ. of Chicago Press, 1984; for a critical examination of its connection to the development of interactionist sociology and methodology, see N. K. Denzin, *Symbolic Interactionism and Cultural Studies*, Blackwell, 1992.

CODING   To begin the process of analyzing the large volume of data generated in the form of transcripts, fieldnotes, photographs, and the like, the qualitative inquirer engages in the activity of coding. Coding is a procedure that disaggregates the data, breaks it down into manageable segments and identifies or names those segments. Although it is impossible to identify and name without at least an implicit conceptual structure, coding is often classified as relatively descriptive *or* analytical/explanatory depending on the degree of interpretation involved. Coding requires constantly comparing and contrasting various successive segments of the data and subsequently categorizing them. Coding can be accomplished in at least three different ways that can be combined: (1) An a priori, content-specific scheme is first developed from careful study of the problem or topic under investigation and the theoretical interests that drive the inquiry. The codes are derived directly by the social inquirer from the language of the problem area or theoretical field. Data are then examined and sorted into this scheme. (2) An a priori, noncontent-specific scheme is developed and data are sorted into the scheme. Noncontent-specific schemes are ways of accounting for the data by sorting it into a typology. The typology may be based on common sense reasoning (e.g., type of event, time of occurrence, participants involved, reactions of participants, physical setting) or derived from the assumptions of a particular methodological framework like symbolic interactionism (e.g., practices, episodes, encounters, roles, relationships; see J. Lofland and L. H. Lofland, *Analyzing Social Settings*, 3rd ed., Wadsworth, 1995). (3) A grounded, a posteriori, inductive, context-sensitive scheme. This scheme may also begin with a simple typology but here analysts (a) work with the actual language of respondents to generate the codes or categories and (b) work back and forth between the data segments and the codes or categories to refine the meaning of categories as they proceed through the data. Depending on the approach taken to coding, the process of coding can yield either a fully labeled (coded) set of data that can be retrieved and manipulated for further analysis or new data documents (e.g., analytical memos, graphic displays) that become the stuff for further analysis (see, for example, M. B. Miles and A. M. Huberman, *Qualitative Data Analysis*, 2nd ed., Sage, 1994). Qualitative data can be coded for the purpose of generating theories and concepts as well as for testing hypotheses.

Perhaps the three most troublesome tendencies to be aware of in coding are (1) the tendency to code largely at the descriptive level rather than to code for the purposes of explaining or developing an understanding of 'what's going on here.' In his discussion of the elaborate coding procedures involved in a *grounded theory* approach, Anselm Strauss (*Qualitative Analysis for Social Scientists,* Cambridge Univ. Press, 1987) advises coding for conditions, interaction among actors, strategies and tactics, and consequences as a way to push coding to the explanatory level; (2) the tendency to think of coding as a mechanical, straightforward, algorithmic process, thereby ignoring the prior conceptualization and theoretical understandings that are involved; (3) the tendency to regard codes or categories as 'fixed' or unchanging labels, thereby ignoring their organic, dynamic character. **See also ANALYZING QUALITATIVE DATA, COMPUTER-ASSISTED DATA ANALYSIS, MEMOING.**

COMPUTER-ASSISTED DATA ANALYSIS This is a growing subfield of a larger movement concerned with technological innovation in qualitative inquiry. New audio recording devices, laptop computers, portable high-quality video cameras, and software for data analysis and visual imaging are making possible new procedures for generating and analyzing qualitative data. The introduction of computer software for facilitating qualitative data analysis coincides with and is partially responsible for the concern about developing rigorous, systematic methods of processing data. Software tools are used for recording, storing, indexing, cross-indexing, coding, sorting, and so on. They facilitate the management of large volumes of data and enable the analyst to locate, label (categorize or code), cross-reference, and compile various combinations of segments of textual data. In some discussions of software tools for data analysis, the implicit assumption often seems to be that because computer-managed analysis is by definition more algorithmic, systematic, and rigorous it is, therefore, better. Although computer-assisted tools make qualitative inquiry a different practice, 'different' is not synonymous with 'better.' One need not be a neo-Luddite to be concerned about how the introduction of these tools contributes to the definition of the discursive practice called qualitative inquiry. As Neil Postman (*Technopoly*, Vintage, 1993) reminds us, embedded in every tool is an ideological bias, a predisposition to construct the world to which the tool will be applied as one thing rather than another. Whereas developers and frequent users of qualitative analysis tools may customarily reflect on these embedded predispositions, it is not entirely clear that the casual user does. The operations made possible by software are not neutral tools, but rather they structure the undertaking of qualitative inquiry. John Seidel, the developer of ETHNOGRAPH™ notes that the following dangers accompany the benefits of software tools: (1) an infatuation with the volume of data one can deal with, leading to sacrificing resolution for scope; (2) a reification of the relationship between researcher and data wherein the researcher assumes that data are 'things out there' that can in a relatively simple and straightforward manner be discovered, identified, collected, counted, and sorted, thereby ignoring the fact that data are artifacts of complex processes of identifying, naming, indexing, and coding that, in turn, are shaped by theoretical and methodological assumptions; (3) a distancing of the researcher from the data (see "Method and Madness in the Application of Computer Technology to Qualitative Data Analysis" in N. G. Fielding and R. M. Lee, *Using Computers in Qualitative Research*, Sage, 1991). For additional information on software for qualitative data analysis, see R. Tesch, *Qualitative Research: Analysis Types and Software Tools*, Falmer, 1990; E. Weitzman and M. B. Miles, *Computer Programs for Qualitative Data Analysis*, Sage, 1994. **See also** CODING, FIELD-NOTES.

CONFIRMABILITY   See TRUSTWORTHINESS CRITERIA.

CONSTANT COMPARISON, METHOD OF   See GROUNDED THEORY
METHODOLOGY.

CONSTRUCTIVISM   This is a philosophical perspective interested in
the ways in which human beings individually and collectively interpret or construct the social and psychological world in specific
linguistic, social, and historical contexts. There are two general
strands of constructivist thought. One strand focuses more on the
individual knower and acts of cognition. Known as 'radical constructivism,' it is represented in the work of Ernst von Glasersfeld
("An Introduction to Radical Constructivism," in P. Watzlawick, ed.,
The Invented Reality, Norton, 1984). Radical constructivism often
claims it is indebted to the genetic *epistemology* of Jean Piaget
(1896-1980). Although Piaget is perhaps better known for his work
in developmental psychology, he did considerable work in theory of
knowledge. He rejected both *empiricism* and *rationalism* and, like
Kant (1724-1804), held that knowledge of the world is mediated by
cognitive structures. Unlike Kant, however, Piaget did not consider
these structures to be given a priori but rather viewed them as the
products of a process of construction resulting from the interaction
of mind and environment (see his *Introduction à l'epistemologie
génétique*, 3 vols., 1950; *The Origins of Intelligence in Children*, Norton,
1952).

A second strand of constructivism focuses more on social process and interaction and is generally known as 'social constructionism.' It is represented, for example, in the work of John Shotter
(*Conversational Realities*, Sage, 1993) and Kenneth Gergen (*Toward
Transformation in Social Knowledge*, 2nd ed., Sage, 1994); see also T. R.
Sarbin and J. I. Kitsue, eds., *Constructing the Social*, Sage, 1994. Social
constructionism has great affinity with theories of symbolic interactionism and *ethnomethodology* that emphasize the actor's definition of the situation; that seek to understand how social actors
recognize, produce, and reproduce social actions, and how they
come to share an intersubjective understanding of specific life circumstances. The classic work in this area is Peter Berger and Thomas
Luckmann's *The Social Construction of Reality* (Doubleday, 1966).
Social constructionism, *symbolic interactionism,* ethogenic social

psychology (R. Harré and P. Secord, *The Explanation of Social Behavior,* Blackwell, 1972), and discursive psychology (R. Harré and G. Gillet, *The Discursive Mind,* Sage, 1994) all share an interest in humans as active agents and constructors of meaning. Yet, the work of Harré is grounded in realist theory of science. Social constructionism is also a significant intellectual thread in the social study of science, particularly in so-called 'laboratory studies' that investigate the ways scientific knowledge is constructed and produced. These studies do not conclude that there is no material reality 'out there' that is studied by natural scientists. Rather, they are interested in examining how that reality is transcribed by the activities of scientists (see K. K. Cetina, *The Manufacture of Knowledge: An Essay on the Constructivist and Contextual Nature of Science,* Pergamon, 1981, and her essay "Laboratory Studies: The Cultural Approach to the Study of Science," in S. Jasanoff et al., eds., *Handbook of Science and Technology,* Sage, 1995).

In general, constructivists reject scientific *realism*—the view that our theories chart, map, or refer to real features of the world—and scientific objectivity—when it is defined as accurate representation of the way the world really is. In contrast, constructivists hold that knowledge of the world is not a simple reflection of what there is, but a set of social artifacts; a reflection of what we make of what is there. Sociobehavioral theories and concepts (e.g., schizophrenia, altruism, disability, mental illness, family, domestic violence, gender, childhood) that we use to refer to the social-political world are (at least in social constructionism) linguistic products of historically situated interactions. Diana Fuss (*Essentially Speaking: Feminism, Nature, and Difference,* Routledge, 1989, p. 3) summarizes this idea as follows: "What is at stake for the constructionist are systems of representations, social and material practices, laws of discourses, and ideological effects. In short, constructionists are concerned above all with the production and organization of differences, and they therefore reject the idea that any essential or natural givens precede the process of social determination." Although these understandings of the world are socially constructed, they are nonetheless real and constitute forms of social action (see, for example, the examination of the effects of the social construction of single mothers and their children in V. Polakow, *Lives on the Edge,* Univ. of Chicago Press, 1993).

CONTENT ANALYSIS   A generic name for a variety of means of textual analysis that involve comparing, contrasting, and categorizing a corpus of data. The data may be cultural artifacts (texts of various kinds, documents, records, billboards, television shows, films, advertisements, and so forth) or events. Classic context analysis emphasized systematic, objective, quantitative description of content derived from researcher-developed categories (see, for example, B. Berelson, *Content Analysis in Communication Research*, Free Press, 1952; K. Krippendorf, *Content Analysis: An Introduction to Its Methodology*, Sage, 1980; R. P. Weber, *Basic Content Analysis*, 2nd ed., Sage, 1990). Contemporary forms of content analysis include, however, both numeric and interpretive means of analyzing data (see, for example, the chapter on content analysis in S. Reinharz, *Feminist Methods in Social Research*, Oxford Univ. Press, 1992).

CONTEXT OF DISCOVERY/CONTEXT OF JUSTIFICATION   See JUDGMENT, LOGICAL EMPIRICISM, TACIT (PERSONAL) KNOWLEDGE.

CONVERSATION ANALYSIS   See ETHNOMETHODOLOGY.

COVERING-LAW MODEL OF EXPLANATION   See EXPLANATION.

CREDIBILITY   See TRUSTWORTHINESS CRITERIA.

CRISIS OF REPRESENTATION   Arguably, developing a general understanding of what this crisis involves holds the key to understanding contemporary forms of qualitative inquiry that seek to break from traditional practice. This phrase was coined by George Marcus and Michael Fischer in *Anthropology as Cultural Critique* (Univ. of Chicago Press, 1986) to refer specifically to the uncertainty within the human sciences about adequate means of describing social reality. The crisis is part of a more general set of ideas across the human sciences that challenge long-standing beliefs about the role of encompassing, generalizing (theoretical, methodological, and political) frameworks that guide empirical research within a discipline. Symptoms of the crisis include the borrowing of ideas and methods across disciplines (e.g., social sciences to literature, literature to philosophy, philosophy to social science), questioning the dominance of post–World War II frameworks and theories that guided inquiry (e.g., Parsonian sociology, Marxism, French structuralism), and the general turn away from developing theoretical models of social and natural order to debates about epistemology, method, forms of representation, and the like. Although foreshadowed and shaped in the antipositivist writing of German scholars in the late nineteenth and early twentieth century, these are the sets of ideas that, over the past three decades, have come to characterize the postmodern condition of the social sciences (and related conditions in literature, philosophy, arts, architecture, and so on). **See also POSTMODERNISM, REPRESENTATION.**

CRITERIA   Criteria for qualitative inquiry are standards, benchmarks, and in some cases regulative ideals, that guide judgments about the goodness or 'quality' of inquiry processes and findings. Criteria that have been proposed for social inquiry include truth, relevance, validity, credibility, plausibility, generalizability, and action/change, among others. Some of these criteria are epistemic (i.e., concerned with justifying knowledge claims as true), others are political (i.e., concerned with warranting the power, use, and effects of knowledge claims or the inquiry process more generally), and still others are moral or ethical standards (i.e., concerned with the right conduct of the inquirer and the inquiry process in general). Criteria are often confused with procedures designed to attain criteria or meet standards. Thus, for example, *analytic induction* (a procedure for testing hypotheses in fieldwork) is a means of demonstrating that the criterion of validity has been met. **See also PROBLEM OF CRITERIA.**

CRITICAL ETHNOGRAPHY   There are two somewhat distinct ways in which the term 'critical' is used here, or perhaps we might say two different kinds of critique. In a more narrow sense, "critical ethnography" refers to ethnographic studies that engage in cultural critique by examining larger political, social, and economic issues and that focus on oppression, conflict, struggle, power, and praxis. As J. VanMaanen (*Tales of the Field,* Univ. of Chicago Press, 1988) points out, these studies are critical of the parochial, romantic, and limited vision of traditional ethnographies. Critical ethnographies of this kind are often, although not necessarily, informed by Marxist and post-Marxist theory. Examples include J. Nash, *We Eat the Mines and the Mines Eat Us* (Columbia Univ. Press, 1979); P. Willis, *Learning to Labour* (Columbia Univ. Press, 1981); G. Nelson and L. Grossman, eds., *Marxism and the Interpretation of Culture* (Univ. of Illinois Press, 1988). In a broader sense, "critical ethnography" refers to the postmodern critique of both classical and interpretive ethnography. Postmodern ethnography criticizes classical ethnography for privileging participant observation, for its tendency to assume a smooth link between 'being there' and understanding the natives' point of view, and for its effort to develop seamless, comprehensive descriptions of common material culture and perspectives. Interpretive ethnography is criticized for privileging *thick description* and for assuming that the ethnographer's understanding can unproblematically reflect that viewpoint of the 'Other.' Central concerns in the postmodern ethnographic critique include the connections between authorship, authority, representation, and rhetoric and an effort to experiment with textual forms for ethnography that decenter the monologic voice of the ethnographer in favor of dialogic or polyphonic texts. For an empirical example, see M. Shostak, *Nisa: The Life and Words of a !Kung Woman* (Harvard Univ. Press, 1981); for a review of the central issues in the postmodern ethnographic critique see J. Clifford and G. Marcus, eds., *Writing Culture: The Poetics and Politics of Ethnography* (Univ. of California Press, 1986). **See also** CRISIS OF REPRESENTATION.

CRITICAL HERMENEUTICS   Also known as 'depth hermeneutics,' this version of *hermeneutics* is explained by Karl Otto-Apel and Jürgen Habermas as well as other critical theorists. It is characterized by several general ideas: (1) It is highly skeptical about given meanings and interpretations. It is suspicious of claims to truth and knowledge and seeks to demystify those claims by engaging in a critique of ideologies that distort understanding and communication. (2) It is emphatically normative; that is, its critiques of meanings and practices are undertaken for the purposes of transforming society and emancipating individuals from false consciousness such that undistorted communication and nonideological understandings can be realized. (3) It is materialist—it is concerned not simply with the relationship between language and meaning and understanding but with concrete, empirical economic, social, organizational, and political conditions and practices that shape human beings as knowers and as social agents. Critical hermeneutics often draws on psychoanalysis as a model for the hermeneutic task, integrating both causal explanation and interpretive self-understanding. **See also CRITICAL SOCIAL SCIENCE.**

C

CRITICAL SOCIAL SCIENCE Generally, this is the research program undertaken by a variety of social theorists that are strongly influenced by critical theory. Critical theory of society, in turn, can be characterized as a blend of practical philosophy and explanatory social science, sharing and radically reforming the intentions of both (Seyla Benhabib, *Critique, Norm, and Utopia: A Study of the Foundations of Critical Theory*, Columbia Univ. Press, 1986). Practical philosophy is concerned with the specifics of ethical and political life (praxis) and the actions that must be undertaken to achieve the good life; explanatory social science produces scientific knowledge of the general causes of *social action.* Critical social science is characterized by several general themes: (1) Its aim, broadly conceived, is to integrate theory and practice in such a way that individuals and groups become aware of the contradictions and distortions in their belief systems and social practices and are then inspired to change those beliefs and practices. Its method here is immanent critique, which challenges belief systems and social relations not by comparing them to some set of external standards but by showing that these practices do not measure up to their own standards and are internally inconsistent, hypocritical, incoherent, and hence comprise a false consciousness. (2) Critical social science is thus practical and normative and not merely descriptive. It rejects the idea of a *disinterested social scientist* and is oriented toward social and individual transformation. (3) It is foregrounded in a critique of instrumental, technical reason. Critical theorists (among other social theorists) argue that this kind of means-end reasoning is pervasive; it informs the traditional empirical-analytic sciences and dominates not only societal processes and cultural meaning but the dynamics of personality formation. Critical social scientists argue that instrumental reason aims to eliminate crises, conflict, and critique. Although founded in the Enlightenment's bid to liberate people from myth, ignorance, and oppression, the 'rationalization' of social and individual life by means of instrumental reason actually works to suppress the very self-transformative, self-reflexive, critical, liberating impulses on which it was founded. Critical inquiry supports a kind of reasoning that is practical, moral, and ethically and politically informed. (4) Thus, to retain or recapture the Enlightenment belief in the power of human reason to affect individual and social transformation, critical social science argues that a form of inquiry is needed that fosters enlightened self-knowledge and effective social-political action. The logic of critical social inquiry requires linking hermeneutic and explanatory social scientific interests (see, for example, D. E. Comstock, "A Method for Critical Research" reprinted in M. Martin and L. C. MacIntyre, eds., *Readings in the Philosophy of Social Science*, MIT Press, 1994). This feature of critical social science—its bid to combine explanatory, hermeneutic, and normative inquiry—marks it as distinctly different from social science characterized by *naturalism* and *antinaturalism* (see B. Fay and J. D. Moon, "What Would an Adequate Philosophy of Social Science Look Like?" in the edited collection noted previously). (5) Critical social science is self-reflexive. To prevent a critical theory of society from becoming yet another self-serving ideology, the theory must account for its own conditions of possibility and their transformative effects. For a discussion of different contemporary interpretations of critical theory and its affiliations with theories of the *Frankfurt school, philosophical hermeneutics,* and *poststructuralism,* see D. C. Hoy and T. McCarthy, *Critical Theory,* Blackwell, 1994. **See also FRANKFURT SCHOOL, INTEREST.**

CROSS-CASE ANALYSIS   (Also called comparative case method or comparative analysis.) A study can include the examination of one case or a collection of cases to learn something about a concept, theory, social process, and so on. Cross-case or comparative approaches include functional analysis as first developed by Durkheim (1858-1917), Marx's (1818-1883) theory of modes of production in societies, and Weber's (1864-1920) methods of historical comparison using ideal types; contemporary methods of quasi-experimentation using multivariate statistical analysis (e.g., T. D. Cook and D. Campbell, *Quasi-Experimentation: Design and Analysis Issues for Field Settings,* Rand McNally, 1979); and, *metaethnography.* In cross-case analysis, two central issues are (1) the rationale for the selection of multiple cases in a single study and (2) the procedures for analyzing data across the cases.

Robert Yin (*Case Study Research*, rev. ed., Sage, 1989, pp. 46-59) advises that the choice of single or multiple cases is a design decision. Cases are rarely if ever chosen as a sample of some universe of cases. Rather, a single-case design is chosen because the case is thought to be critical to the elaboration or test of a theory, extreme or unique, or unusually revelatory. The choice of multiple-case designs (permitting cross-case analysis) follows what Yin calls a replication rather than a sampling logic: Additional cases are chosen for study because such cases are expected to yield similar information or findings or contrary but predictable findings. Robert Stake (*The Art of Case Study Research*, Sage, 1995, pp. 3-6) agrees that cases are not chosen for representativeness. He describes the "instrumental case study" as strategy whereby a case is studied because it can shed light on a particular pregiven issue, concept, or problem. When several cases are chosen within a single study to achieve this aim, each is thought to be useful in that regard. The result is what he calls a "collective case study."

Procedures for examining and displaying a wide variety of qualitative data across multiple cases are explored in Matthew Miles and A. Michael Huberman (*Qualitative Data Analysis*, 2nd ed., Sage, 1994). C. C. Ragin (*The Comparative Method: Moving Beyond Qualitative and Quantitative Strategies*, Univ. of California Press, 1987) discusses methods of combining both qualitative and quantitative data in comparative analysis. **See also** CASE STUDY RESEARCH, CODING, METAETHNOGRAPHY, SAMPLING.

CULTURE   What constitutes culture and how it is best described and interpreted is a matter of much debate. There is little overall consensus on its precise meaning. In *ethnography*, culture is used as an analytic not as a descriptive term. In other words, the term does not describe a set of traits of a group but refers to a form or pattern abstracted from observed behavior. Yet, it is not clear whether this abstraction is an ideal type, norm, mean, or so on. Two very broad ways of using the term "culture" analytically are as an ideational system—a system of knowledge and concepts—and as a material system—the sum of physical artifacts, technologies, and so on—of a particular group. Culture can be framed in terms of meaning, symbolism, language, and discourse drawing respectively on phenomenology, cultural anthropology, structuralism, semiotics, and critical theory (see R. Wuthnow et al., eds., *Cultural Analysis,* Routledge & Kegan Paul, 1984). It can also be viewed through functionalist, dramaturgical, Weberian, Durkheimian, Marxist, and poststructural perspectives (see J. C. Alexander and S. Seidman, eds., *Culture and Society: Contemporary Debates,* Cambridge Univ. Press, 1990).

C

DATA MANAGEMENT, STORAGE, RETRIEVAL Simply put, field-work generates lots of 'stuff,' and the longer one is engaged in the field, the more stuff one accumulates—tapes of interviews, audio-tape transcripts, fieldnotes, personal notes, notes on readings, photographs, copies of documents, and so forth. An absolutely essential task for any fieldworker is designing a system for organizing, cataloging, and indexing these materials that makes it possible to retrieve them efficiently and use them for different tasks. The system one designs will, in turn, affect the way one conceptualizes the process of analyzing the data. Some practical principles of design are discussed in M. Miles and A. M. Huberman, *Qualitative Data Analysis*, 2nd ed., Sage, 1994, pp. 45ff.

DECONSTRUCTIONISM The kind of *hermeneutics* practiced in *post-structuralism*, also called radical hermeneutics and the *hermeneu-*

tics of suspicion. The term 'Destrucktion' was originally explained by Martin Heidegger (1889-1976), although Jacques Derrida's term 'deconstruction' is the most often cited source (*Of Grammatology*, trans. G. Spivak, Johns Hopkins, 1976; *Writing and Difference*, Routledge and Kegan Paul, 1987; *Positions*, Univ. of Chicago Press, 1981). Derrida strongly objected to what he called the logocentrism or logocentric bias of Western thought. He argued that there is no interior 'language' of thought and intention such that the sense and referent of a term is determined by its nature. Terms conceived as 'naturally' referring to something are called logi (from the Greek *logos*). Any account (explanation) of the world that presupposes such terms is logocentric. This kind of account both assigns to and demands reverence for the knower's words: "The presumption [is] that words reflect the workings of the mind as it converts the surrounding chaos into logical order" (K. Gergen, *The Saturated Self*, Basic Books, 1991, p. 107). Derrida argued that once we recognize the logocentricity of all accounts of the natural and social world, then language is only an endless play of signifiers (see *semiotics*) with indeterminate meaning, and thought and intention are merely wordlike and have no intrinsic connection to some referent (see the entry "Deconstruction" in R. Audi, general ed., *The Cambridge Dictionary of Philosophy*, Cambridge Univ. Press, 1995). The aim of deconstructionism is thus not to decode a *text* to somehow reveal its meaning or truth but to demystify it; to displace or unsettle its taken-for-granted concepts like the unity of the text, the meaning or message of the text, the authorship of the text. As Pauline Rosenau (*Postmodernism and the Social Sciences*, Princeton Univ. Press, 1992, p. 120) explains, deconstructionism "involves demystifying a text, tearing it apart to reveal its internal hierarchies and its presuppositions [e.g., author-text; object-subject; right-wrong, and so on]. It lays out the flaws and the latent metaphysical structures of a text [e.g., unity, identity, meaning, authorship]. A deconstructive reading of a text seeks to discover its ambivalence, blindness, logocentricity . . . [it] examines what is left out of a text, what is unnamed, what is excluded, and what is concealed." The act of deconstruction takes place within the terms that have shaped the text; it does not stand outside of the text but unfolds within the position being discussed in the text itself. Deconstruction of a text is not undertaken for the

purposes of revealing its errors or showing various different interpretations, for that would assume that there is a 'truth' or meaning
in the text. In this respect, deconstructionism departs from *philosophical hermeneutics* that holds there is a meaning to be constructed in the engagement of the interpreter with the text (see, for
example, the dispute between Derrida and Gadamer in D. P.
Michelfelder and R. E. Palmer, eds., *Dialogue and Deconstruction: The
Gadamer-Derrida Exchange,* SUNY Press, 1989). Deconstructionism
shares with *critical hermeneutics* a suspicion of what purports to be
the truth and thus seeks to unmask this erroneous assumption. But
unlike critical hermeneutics, radical hermeneutics or deconstructionism holds out little hope for achieving emancipation from ideologically distorted meanings. Quite simply, there is nothing more to
interpretations than the endless plays of words. For an example of a
deconstructive reading see Norman K. Denzin, "Postmodernism
and Deconstructionism" in David R. Dickens and Andrea Fontana,
eds., *Postmodernism and Social Theory,* Guilford, 1994.

DEDUCTION   See INFERENCE.

DEDUCTIVE-NOMOLOGICAL EXPLANATION   See EXPLANATION.

DEPENDABILITY   See TRUSTWORTHINESS CRITERIA.

DESCRIPTION   See THICK DESCRIPTION.

DESCRIPTIVE STATISTICS   These are mathematical techniques used
for the purposes of organizing, displaying, and summarizing a set
of numerical data. They include measures of central tendency (mean,
median, and mode) and measures of variability (standard devia-
tion). It is not at all uncommon for field studies to report the results
of community or group surveys using descriptive statistics.

DESKWORK   A phrase coined by John VanMaanen (*Tales of the Field:
On Writing Ethnography,* Univ. of Chicago Press, 1988) to indicate a
phase of qualitative work different from tasks completed while in
the field. It refers to the activities of organizing, sense making,
analyzing, and interpreting of field notes and the writing up of the
study that takes place after one leaves the field.

DISCOURSE ANALYSIS A general term covering a variety of approaches to the analysis of recorded talk; sometimes used interchangeably with conversation analysis (but for a brief summary of differences between the two approaches see H. Silverman, *Interpreting Qualitative Data: Methods for Analyzing Talk, Text, and Interaction*, Sage, 1993). Discourse analysis is an interdisciplinary approach drawing on insights from ethnomethodology, sociolinguistics, cognitive psychology, communication studies, and ordinary language philosophy. It is principally concerned with the analysis of the process of communication itself. It draws on insights of speech-act theory developed by the philosopher J. L. Austin (*How to Do Things with Words*, Clarendon Press, 1962). Austin argued that language is not best understood either as an expression of the speaker's underlying cognitive state or as describing some state of affairs. Rather, language is a performance; speech or utterances perform an action. Discourse analysts seek to understand the action(s) that various kinds of talk 'performs.' **See also** ETHNOMETHODOLOGY.

DISCOURSE THEORY Postmodern discourse theory defines all social phenomena as structured semiotically by codes and rules and therefore amenable to linguistic analysis using semiotic concepts, for example: sign, expression, content, interpretant, codes, and so on (see, for example, S. Best & D. Kellner, *Postmodern Theory*, Guilford, 1991, pp. 17-21, 26-27). This theory challenges and often encompasses previous semiotic theories and informs several versions of qualitative inquiry (see, for example, the discussion of sociosemiotics in M. Gottdiener, "Semiotics and Postmodernism" in D. R. Dickens and A. Fontana, eds., *Postmodernism and Social Inquiry*, Guilford, 1994). **See also** POSTSTRUCTURALISM, SEMIOTICS.

DISCURSIVE PRACTICE This refers to particular ways of talking and writing about and doing or performing one's *practice* that are coupled with particular social settings in which those ways of talking are regarded as understandable and more or less valuable. To refer to qualitative inquiry as a discursive practice (or a set of discursive practices) is to acknowledge that the language of the practice is in part constitutive of its meaning and that the meaning and significance of the practice is reflective of the intentions of its practitioners as well as socially, historically, and politically constructed. Discursive practices and the languages of practices function as signs of social identity and difference for their practitioners. Discursive inquiry practices are at once ethical and political and not simply technical undertakings.

DISINTERESTED SOCIAL SCIENCE/SCIENTIST   Owing in large part to the legacy of Max Weber (1864-1920), Western social science generally endorses the idea that social scientists as scientists should be disinterested observers of the social-political world. They should study the workings of society dispassionately and aim only at developing and testing theoretical *explanations* of the way the world is. Judgments about the way the social-political world ought to be should be left to others to decide. The enterprise of social science and the individual social scientist should be value free, that is, neutral with respect to decisions about how we should live or act as humans in society. Social science can be relevant to decisions about values, but only by empirically demonstrating consequences of different means to various ends or by describing and explaining the values and norms held by members of a society. This posture or doctrine does not mean that science has no values whatsoever: The scientific enterprise values dispassionate, objective investigation of scientific claims and the idea of a scientifically informed (but neutral with respect to social norms) policy making. For a summary of this view and alternatives see R. J. Bernstein, *The Restructuring of Social and Political Theory*, Univ. of Pennsylvania Press, 1976; M. Root, *Philosophy of Social Science*, Blackwell, 1993. This separation of empirical explanatory theory from normative concerns (a sharp distinction between the 'is' and the 'ought,' or between scientific claims about social phenomena and practical-moral discourse, or the heterogeneity of facts and values) in the work of the social inquirer is challenged by a variety of different philosophies of social inquiry including *participatory action research,* some feminist methodologies, *critical social science,* and some versions of *philosophical hermeneutics.* **See also MULTIPLE REALITIES, POLITICS OF RESEARCH, PRAXIS.**

DOCUMENT ANALYSIS   Refers broadly to various procedures involved in analyzing and interpreting data generated from the examination of documents and records relevant to a particular study. These sources of data can include public records (e.g., political and judicial reports, government documents, media accounts, television scripts, yearbooks, minutes of meetings); private documents (e.g., medical histories, letters, diaries, school records, personal journals, memoirs); interview transcripts and transcripts prepared from video records, photographs, and so on. The literature on document analysis also addresses a variety of issues concerning obtaining access to records and documents and examining their authenticity. **See also** CONTENT ANALYSIS, LIFE-HISTORY METHODOLOGY.

D

DOUBLE HERMENEUTIC   This term was coined by the social theorist Anthony Giddens (*The Constitution of Society: Outline of a Theory of Structuration,* Univ. of California Press, 1984). Giddens argues that the double hermeneutic characterizes the social sciences and serves to distinguish them from the natural sciences. The social scientist studies phenomena (i.e., social actions of various kinds), which (unlike the objects studied in natural science) are already constituted as meaningful. Humans are 'concept-using' beings whose concepts of their action help constitute what those actions are and what they mean. Hence, the first task of the social inquirer is to understand the concepts of the social actors that are the object of study. That is, the inquirer must first get to know the world of the actors, what they already know and have to know to 'go on' with their daily social activity. From this first-level understanding, social inquirers construct second-order concepts and theories to explain what social actors are doing. Yet, these second-order concepts of the social scientist can, in turn, actually become first-order concepts as they are appropriated and interpreted by social actors. In other words, the concepts and theories of the social inquirer can circulate in and out of the very social world that those concepts were first invented to analyze and explain. Social scientific theory and concepts, unlike those in natural science, can actually alter the way society behaves. There is thus a double process of interpretation.

EMERGENT DESIGN This is an unfortunate term for an important idea. Fieldworkers routinely adjust their inquiry plans and strategies in response to what they are learning in the field site. For example, a fieldworker may discover documents of particular importance that she was not aware existed; come across particular respondents who need to be interviewed when this was not anticipated; identify and cultivate a relationship with a key informant where that may have been thought impossible; decide after a study is already under way to conduct a community survey to gather a broader picture of an issue; and so on. Hence, in contrast to, for example, the plans for a quasi-experimental study that would be worked out in detail in advance of actually conducting the study (from precise specification of hypotheses, through selection of groups, to choice and pretesting of measures and specification of procedures for the statistical analysis of data, and so forth), a field study is often (although not necessarily) not so precisely planned in advance. By both allowing for and anticipating changes in strategies, procedures, ways of generating data, and so on, the fieldworker seeks to make her or his plans (i.e., 'design') responsive to the circumstances of the particular study. Often, this responsive characteristic of planning and conducting a field study is referred to as emergent design. If we use the strict sense of the word "emergent" (i.e., arising unexpectedly), it would be reasonable to say that the fieldworker does encounter emergent issues, emergent circumstances that call for a response, or both, and hence the plan for fieldwork ought to flexible and adaptive. As a modifier for "design," however, the term "emergent" can suggest that the design itself arises unexpectedly or that the fieldworker has no design or plan at all at the outset of the study. This kind of complete laissez-faire attitude of seeing 'what happens' is ill advised. The fieldworker seeks to understand and portray some problem, event, issue, concept, life, and so on and should have given careful thought in advance of undertaking the fieldwork how that understanding can best be developed and how claims made about a social phenomenon can be warranted. **See also** SENSITIZING CONCEPTS.

EMIC/ETIC Originating in linguistics (phon<u>emic</u> v. phon<u>etic</u>), a distinction between emic and etic cultural categories was once popular in cognitive anthropology. Emic terms were indigenous—specific to a language or culture—whereas etic terms were developed by the social inquirer and used to describe and compare sociocultural systems. Etic terms were used by cognitive anthropology and other formalist approaches to ethnography as something like a codebook of concepts facilitating cross-cultural comparisons. This absolute distinction has been severely criticized on the grounds that there are no purely etic categories unbound to some specific context. Interest in distinguishing inside from outside perspectives remains although it is now recognized that these distinctions are relative. The terms "emic" and "etic" are still occasionally used more broadly: emic to refer to first-order concepts—the local language, concepts, or ways of expression used by members in a particular group or setting to name their experience; etic to refer to second-order concepts—the scientific language used by the social scientist to refer to the same phenomena. In his essay "From the Native's Point of View: On the Nature of Anthropological Understanding" (reprinted in C. Geertz, *Local Knowledge*, Basic Books, 1983, pp. 55-70), the interpretive anthropologist Clifford Geertz introduced the concepts experience-near and experience-distant as a refinement of the emic-etic distinction. An experience-near concept is one that a respondent or informant "might naturally and effortlessly use to define what he [sic] or his fellows see, feel, think, imagine, and . . . which he would readily understand when similarly applied by others"; an experience-distant concept is one "that specialists of one sort or another . . . employ to forward their scientific, philosophical, or practical aims." Geertz explained that both kinds of concepts are necessary in ethnographic analysis because "Confinement to experience-near concepts leaves the ethnographer awash in immediacies, as well as entangled in vernacular. Confinement to experience-distant ones leaves him [sic] stranded in abstractions and smothered in jargon." Geertz uses these concepts to defend the methodology of participant observation as a dialectic of experience and interpretation: He stresses the importance of grasping insider's perspectives through experience-near concepts while simultaneously illuminating their connection to experience-distant concepts (see J. Clifford, "On Ethnographic Authority," *Representations*, 1983, 1(2), p. 127). **See also NATIVE'S POINT OF VIEW.**

EMPIRICAL RESEARCH   Qualitative inquiry, including case study, ethnography, life history, oral history and the like, is empirical research because it deals with the data of experience. Its claims are based on the evidence of observations, both those of the inquirer and the reports of people studied, that rely on the senses. When a qualitative inquirer makes a claim (assertion, statement, working hypothesis, and so forth) about an event, object, process, person, or so on and offers as evidence or warrant for that claim its relationship to experience (something the inquirer or respondents saw or heard), then that inquirer is engaging in empirical inquiry. To assert, however, that qualitative inquiry is empirical research is not to assert that it is "empiricist" in orientation. The term "empiricist" carries a negative connotation. It usually refers to someone who believes that the data of experience are the foundation of all knowledge claims and that only empirical observations (not reason) can be trusted. **See also EMPIRICISM, RATIONALISM.**

EMPIRICISM   This is the name for a family of theories of epistemology that generally accept the premise that knowledge begins with sense experience. This view of epistemology is often contrasted with *rationalism,* which holds that reason is the primary way of acquiring knowledge. Defenders of empiricism (including David Hume (1711-1776), the logical positivists of the Vienna Circle, and contemporary empiricists like W. V. O. Quine) do not argue that knowledge is somehow 'given' in the brute data of experience, such that the inquirer is merely a spectator or passive recording device. On the contrary, empiricists are deeply concerned with the activity of how to construct concepts and theories (i.e., explanations, predictions) out of brute data.

All forms of qualitative inquiry are empirical to the extent that they deal in the data of experience. Yet, the terms "empiricism," "empirical sciences," and "empiricist" are often used to connote a particular kind of social inquiry at odds with so-called qualitative inquiry. This is due in part to the fact that *logical positivism* was inspired by an incredibly strict empiricism and a later version adopted the name *logical empiricism.* A strict empiricist account of knowledge (or strict empiricism) in the social sciences holds that claims about social reality or human action are verifiable with reference to brute data. A brute datum is a piece of evidence expressed as an observation statement that is free of any taint of subjective interpretation and that requires no further interpretation or checking. In brief, the empiricist believes in the possibility of particular kinds of observations (or observation statements) comprising the bedrock of all knowledge claims.

The strict empiricism of logical positivist philosophy was strongly challenged by hermeneutic and phenomenological approaches to the human sciences (see, e.g., Charles Taylor, "Interpretation and the Sciences of Man," *Review of Metaphysics*, 1971, 24: 3-51). Strict empiricism was also the target of attack by historians and philosophers of science called the *Weltanschauung* analysts (e.g., Thomas Kuhn, Stephen Toulmin, Norwood Hanson, Michael Polanyi), who argued that the worldviews (*Weltanschauungen*) of

E

scientists—their prior knowledge, historical circumstances, beliefs, and so on—played a critical role in the testing and justification of scientific claims. **See also** EMPIRICAL RESEARCH, POSTEMPIRICISM.

END OF PHILOSOPHY   The work of Friedrich Nietzsche (1844-1900) is looked to particularly by poststructuralists as having heralded the death of traditional philosophical concerns with clarifying the meaning of truth, reality, morality, virtue, and the like. The existentialist and phenomenological philosophy of fellow German philosopher Martin Heidegger (1889-1976) is also sometimes appealed to in the same way. Heidegger saw philosophy's quest for knowing truth and reality as an illusionary search for foundations outside the province of the individual thinker or knower. Following in the wake and building on the insights of these and other pronouncements of the death of philosophy are a variety of "post" philosophical positions (e.g., *feminist methodology, poststructuralism, critical theory, philosophical hermeneutics*, postanalytic philosophy, neopragmatism) taken up by Sandra Harding, Nancy Fraser, Nancy Harstock, Allison Jaggar, Jacques Derrida, Michel Foucault, Hans-Georg Gadamer, Jürgen Habermas, Jean-François Lyotard, Alasdair MacIntyre, Hilary Putnam, Richard Rorty, and Charles Taylor, to name but a few.

Whether we use the phrase "after philosophy," "end of philosophy," "postanalytic philosophy," or "postphilosophy" matters less than understanding the nature of the turmoil. The collection of essays edited by Kenneth Baynes, James Bohman, and Thomas McCarthy titled *After Philosophy: End or Transformation?* (MIT Press, 1987) argues that this period is characterized by various criticisms of notions that form the core of the Enlightenment tradition: the necessity and universality of reason; the autonomous, disengaged, atomistic, sovereign, rational subject; knowledge as representation; the separation of philosophy from rhetoric and poetics; and so on. The collection edited by John Rajchman and Cornel West, *Postanalytic Philosophy* (Columbia Univ. Press, 1985), emphasizes the "de-disciplinizing" of philosophy and its mergers with literary theory, history of science, and political theory. This period of intellectual debate in philosophy is highly significant for social inquiry in general and for qualitative inquiry in particular. The debate has influenced the way social science philosophers and social scientists and define the nature and aim of social inquiry; the authority, role, and expertise of the inquirer; the epistemological status of claims to represent social reality; and so on. Thus, the contemporary scene in the broad field of qualitative inquiry is philosophically complex and has moved well beyond the tired debate of quantitative versus qualitative methods into far more interesting (and complicated) matters of epistemology and the politics of inquiry. **See also** EPISTE-MOLOGY.

E

EPISTEMIC CRITERION See VALIDITY.

EPISTEMOLOGY This is the study of the nature of knowledge and justification. There are many theories of epistemology. For example, empiricist epistemology argues that knowledge is derived from sense experience. Genuine, legitimate knowledge consists of beliefs that can be justified by observation. The *logical positivists* were thoroughgoing empiricists. Rationalist epistemology argues that reason is the sure path to knowledge. Rationalists may claim that sense experiences are an effect of external causes; that a priori ideas (concepts, theories, and so on) provide a structure for making sense of experience; that reason provides a kind of certainty that the senses cannot provide; or all of these.

Rather than conceiving of the differences between so-called qualitative and quantitative inquiry in terms of tools and methods, students of qualitative inquiry might be better served by examining the differences between epistemologies, for example, the epistemologies of empiricism and hermeneutics (see, for example, C. Taylor, "Interpretation and the Sciences of Man," *Review of Metaphysics*, 1971, 25: 3-51) or empiricist and feminist epistemologies (see, for example, L. Alcoff and E. Potter, eds., *Feminist Epistemologies*, Routledge, 1993). Epistemologies provide much of the justification for particular methodologies (i.e., the aim, function and assumptions of method); see, for example, M. Hollis, *The Philosophy of Social Science*, Cambridge Univ. Press, 1994.

Currently, there is much criticism being directed at what is sometimes called the "epistemological project" or "philosophy-as-epistemology." There are two significantly different strands of criticism here that share the same diagnosis but issue in different remedies, so to speak. The diagnosis is that both rationalist and empiricist epistemologies are foundationalist, that is, they seek permanent, indisputable criteria for knowledge—one finds it in reason, the other in sense experience. These epistemologies are also characterized by their interest in an automomous, detached subject (knower) and a preoccupation with establishing correspondence between ideal and object, concept and observation. The 'quest for certainty' characteristic of these epistemologies not only has been found wanting, but is thought to be a futile and dysfunctional search.

Hermeneutic, feminist, poststructuralist, pragmatist, and critical social science approaches to social inquiry all generally accept (and have in various ways made) this diagnosis. Yet, two different responses result. One response is pragmatic and fallibilistic. It holds that knowledge is by definition plural and uncertain and the best we can do is make a stand on the basis of (admittedly fallible) human judgment. This response abandons Epistemology with a capital "E"—the search for the foundations or essences of knowledge—but retains the idea of epistemology with a lower-case "e"—reflection of various kinds about what it means to know. The other response is one of radical skepticism or epistemological nihilism. It holds that diverse realities, plural constructions, the absence of certainty, intertextuality, shifting identities of subjects, and the like all add up to the undecidability of all interpretation. No interpretations, no judgments are decidedly better than any other. This response abandons the whole idea of epistemology or assumes "epistemological impossibilism" (M. Calinescu, *Five Faces of Modernity*, Duke Univ. Press, 1987). **See also** FEMINIST EPISTEMOLOGY, FALLIBILISM, NARRATIVE EPISTEMOLOGY, OBJECTIVISM, PRAGMATISM.

ERKLÄRUNG   This is a German term for "explanation." See EXPLANATION, *VERSTEHEN*.

ESSENTIALISM   This is a metaphysical doctrine that holds that objects have essences, that is, intrinsic identifying or characterizing properties that constitute their real, true nature. Humanism, for example, posits a universal or essential character of "Man." Some feminists argue for essential features of men's and women's biology, identity, and gender. Essentialism is the foil for other feminists and for many constructivists and poststructuralists who argue that plurality, otherness, difference, and heterogeneity characterize our understanding of notions like subject, man, woman, gender, self, family, intelligence, anxiety, and so on. **See also CONSTRUCTIVISM.**

ETHICS OF QUALITATIVE INQUIRY   The ethics of qualitative inquiry, as with other forms of social inquiry, are concerned with the ethical principles and obligations (including their articulation in professional codes) governing conduct in the field and writing up accounts of *fieldwork*. Conventional treatments of ethics attend to the unique kinds of moral dilemmas arising from sustained interpersonal fieldwork and the kinds of ethical frameworks (e.g., utilitarianism, ethical relativism, and so on) and principles (e.g., autonomy, beneficence, and so on) that might provide guidance in reasoning ethically through dilemmas arising from dealing with issues of trust, confidentiality, harm, deception, consent, and so forth (see, for example, M. Bulmer, ed., *Social Research Ethics*, Macmillan, 1982; J. F. Gubrium and D. Silverman, eds., *The Politics of Field Research*, Sage, 1989). The challenge currently being made to traditional conceptions of ethical theory and practice by feminist philosophers (e.g., K. Pyne Addelson, *Moral Passages*, Routledge, 1994; A. C. Baier, *Moral Prejudices*, Harvard Univ. Press, 1994; E. B. Cole and S. Coultrap-McQuin, eds., *Explorations in Feminist Ethics*, Indiana Univ. Press, 1992), postmodern scholarship (e.g., Z. Bauman, *Postmodern Ethics*, Blackwell, 1983), and neo-Aristotelian ethical theory (e.g., B. Williams, *Ethics and the Limits of Philosophy*, Cambridge Univ. Press, 1985; A. MacIntyre, *After Virtue*, Univ. of Notre Dame Press, 1980), however, is beginning to influence thinking about the ethics of fieldwork in particular and of qualitative (and social science) inquiry more generally. Two kinds of developments are occurring. The first has to do with the paradigm of ethical reasoning itself: Emphasis is shifting away from the Kantian universalist and impersonalist tradition of ethics in which ethical understanding or ethical judgment is a matter of the lone moral agent grasping and applying moral principles to specific dilemmas and toward understanding ethics as a search for the various ways in which human beings are dialogically engaged with and respond to each other in their struggles to understand what it is right to do. The second is concerned with introducing new concepts as the basis for moral theory, for example, trust, care, and normative attention (vs. rights, obligations, justice, and so on).

E

ETHNOGRAPHIC NATURALISM   Various interpretations of this doctrine, also called social realism, foreground much of what is identified as qualitative inquiry. A strong interpretation of the doctrine means the inquirer must capture the 'true' or real nature of social phenomena. The more common weak interpretation means respect for or attention to the nature of phenomenon under study. A weak interpretation is evident in the claims of qualitative inquirers who argue that we can (and should) carefully distinguish observations of objective social and physical facts from the interpretations of those facts. Both strong and weak varieties share the core idea that "By entering into close, relatively prolonged contact with people in their everyday lives we can come to understand their beliefs and behaviors more accurately, in a way that would not be possible by means of any other approach" (M. Hammersley, *What's Wrong With Ethnography?*, Routledge, 1992, pp. 43-44). Furthermore, both share the idea of fidelity to phenomenon and reject the idea of fidelity to methodological principles. In other words, the primary commitment of the social inquirer should be to remain true to the nature of the phenomenon under study rather than to honor a particular conception of scientific method. Herbert Blumer (*Symbolic Interactionism*, Prentice Hall, 1969, p. 27) explained this commitment as follows: "Reality exists in the empirical world and not in the methods used to study that world; it is to be discovered in the examination of that world. . . . Methods are mere instruments designed to identify and analyze the obdurate character of this empirical world, and as such their value exists only in their suitability in enabling this task to be done." Ethnographic naturalism typically finds its expression in ethnographic realism. Defenders of postmodern approaches to ethnographic work (e.g., in sociology Norman Denzin and Patricia Clough; in anthropology Stephen Tyler) take strong exception to this doctrine. **See also** ETHNOGRAPHIC REALISM, FIELD, NATURALISTIC INQUIRY, REPRESENTATION.

ETHNOGRAPHIC REALISM   This is the genre of ethnographic writing that reflects the assumptions of ethnographic naturalism. If *ethnography* is both process and product, then traditionally its process of *participant observation* is built on the doctrine of ethnographic naturalism and its product reflects the practice of ethnographic realism.

The genre is composed of a number of literary conventions that contribute to the construction of a representational text, that is, a text that claims to represent literally the ways of life, attitudes, practices, beliefs, and so on of those studied. John VanMaanen (*Tales of the Field*, Univ. of Chicago Press, 1988, pp. 46ff.) identifies the following four conventions as characteristic of these texts or what he calls "realist tales": (1) The experience of the researcher serves as a source of authority, yet the author is virtually completely absent from most segments of the text. VanMaanen notes that "Ironically, by taking the 'I' (observer) out of the ethnographic report, the narrator's authority is apparently enhanced, and audience worries over personal subjectivity become moot." (2) A documentary style is employed, focusing on the mundane details of everyday life and revealing the powers of observation of the inquirer. This catalog of observations is often presented via standard anthropological or sociological categories that typically are used to divide the complex field of others' ways of life into something manageable (e.g., family life, work life, social networks, customs, beliefs, rituals, kinship patterns). Details within these categories are not randomly arranged but accumulate systematically and redundantly to demonstrate something important about respondents' 'lived reality' from the fieldworker's point of view. (3) The native's (respondent's) point of view is painstakingly produced through extensive, closely edited quotations to convey that what is presented is not the fieldworker's view but authentic and representative remarks of respondents. (4) There is a marked absence of reflection on whether the fieldworker got it right, a tendency toward a no-nonsense approach to presenting representations and accounts. VanMaanen calls this the attitude of "interpretive omnipotence" on the part of the author.

Postmodern ethnography (in both sociology and anthropology) has arisen largely as a challenge to the doctrine of ethnographic realism and the production of realist texts. In a variety of ways it questions the notion that fieldwork texts can be direct, matter-of-fact accounts of other's experience unclouded by how the fieldworker produced the product. It experiments with other textual forms that reflect the social dynamics of fieldworker-respondent relations as interlocutory, dialogical, collaborative, and cocreative of understanding the lives of others. **See also** ETHNOGRAPHIC NATURALISM, LITERARY TURN.

ETHNOGRAPHY   The methodology born in anthropology, ethnography is a particular kind of qualitative inquiry distinguishable from case study research, descriptive studies, naturalistic inquiry, and so forth by the fact that it is the process and product of describing and interpreting <u>cultural</u> behavior. Yet, what it has in common with these other kinds of qualitative inquiries is its emphasis on firsthand *field study.* Although there is considerable disagreement in the meaning of the term *"culture,"* both anthropological and sociological definitions of ethnography stress the centrality of culture as the analytic concept that informs the doing of ethnography.

Ethnography unites both process and product, *fieldwork* and written text. Fieldwork, undertaken as *participant observation,* is the process by which the ethnographer comes to know a culture; the ethnographic text is how culture is portrayed. There is general agreement that culture itself is not visible or tangible but is constructed by the act of ethnographic writing. Hence, understanding what it means to 'write' culture (i.e., literal *representation, inscription, transcription, textualization,* cultural translation) is a critical concern in ethnography. The term "ethnography" is often used as a synonym for fieldwork and its characteristics of prolonged time in the *field,* generation of descriptive data, development of rapport and empathy with respondents, the use of multiple data sources, the making of *fieldnotes,* and so forth. But it should be noted that although many kinds of qualitative inquirers may engage in fieldwork, not all do ethnographic fieldwork. **See also** CULTURE.

ETHNOLOGY   The historical-geographical and comparative study of peoples or cultures.

ETHNOMETHODOLOGY   This approach to social inquiry has been described as the study of everyday practical reasoning and as the study of the processes whereby rules that cover interactional settings are constructed. It is a family of related approaches concerned with describing and portraying how people construct their own definitions of a social situation or, more broadly, with the social construction of knowledge. Its originator is Harold Garfinkel (*Studies in*

Ethnomethodology, Prentice Hall, 1967), but it also broadly covers the cognitive sociology of Aaron Cicourel (*Cognitive Sociology,* Free Press, 1974), constitutive ethnography (H. Mehan and H. Wood, *The Reality of Ethnomethodology,* John Wiley, 1975), microethnography (also called ethnography of communication; see examples in G. Spindler, ed., *Doing the Ethnography of Schooling: Educational Anthropology in Action,* Holt, Rinehart and Winston, 1982), and more recent forms of the approach known as conversation analysis that focus on the details of ordinary, mundane, naturally occurring talk to reveal the collaborative practices used by speakers to accomplish intelligible conversation and the norms implicit in conversation (see J. M. Atkinson and J. Heritage, eds., *Structures of Social Action,* Cambridge Univ. Press, 1984; J. Heritage, "Ethnomethodology," in A. Giddens and J. Turner, eds., *Social Theory Today,* Stanford Univ. Press, 1987). One rough way of differentiating various ethnomethodological approaches from one another is to identify how each views language: (1) Is it regarded primarily as means of communication and hence the interest is the analysis of the process of communication per se and the examination of a *transcription* for its content? or (2) Is language regarded more as a manifestation of culture and hence the language of a transcription is analyzed for the purposes of determining how individuals come to a shared understanding of each other and of social situations? Ethnomethodological approaches to social inquiry share (1) a general orientation derived from *phenomenological sociology*—a focus on the ways the *life-world* is produced, experienced, or accomplished interactionally and discursively; (2) a methodological approach that prefers observation focused on (both the audio and visual) recording of micro-exchanges and fine-grained analysis of transcripts of those data; and (3) a commitment to bracket out the researcher's own sense of the way encounters are socially structured or accomplished to describe how members in a specific setting or parties to an interaction accomplish a sense of structure. **See also** DISCOURSE ANALYSIS.

EXPLANATION   In common sense usage, to explain something is to make it intelligible or understandable. But what constitutes an explanation in social inquiry is a matter of much dispute. Two critical issues for qualitative inquiry are: (1) What is an adequate or appropriate theoretical explanation? What is the character of social explanation? (2) Is explanation an appropriate goal for the human or social sciences?

   The nature of theoretical explanation. The most influential, although not universally accepted, view of what constitutes the logic of explanation in the social sciences or an adequate social scientific explanation is the covering-law model. This model explains an event/action by subsuming or covering it under one or more general causal laws. This model has two forms: In the case in which laws are deterministic (universal), a deductive-nomological explanation is possible. This takes the following form:

$L_1, L_2, L_3, \ldots L_n$	(Testable causal laws)
$C_1, C_2, C_3, \ldots C_n$	(Testable statements of background conditions)
———————	
E	(Statement of the event, action to be explained)

In circumstances where laws are statistical (probabilistic), explanation takes an inductive-statistical form:

$L_1, L_2, L_3, \ldots L_n$	(Testable statistical laws)
$C_1, C_2, C_3, \ldots C_n$	(Testable statements of background conditions)
═══════════	
E	(Statement of the event, action to be explained)

In the former, the laws and conditions deductively entail the event or action to be explained by showing why it was necessary under the circumstances. In the latter, laws and conditions help show only why the event or action was probable (not necessary).

   Much controversy surrounds the issue of whether the covering-law model in general is the most appropriate definition of social scientific explanation and what constitutes a legitimate form of an inductive-statistical explanation. Nonetheless, for defenders of *logical empiricism* this is a generally accepted account of what constitutes theoretical explanation. On this view, the goal of social science is to develop social *theory*—a unified causal explanation that ties together laws, generalizations, hypotheses, and so on. Other models or accounts of explanation are also popular in social science, but there is significant debate about whether these models are more or less variations on the kind of causal explanation defended in the covering-law model or simply poor substitutes.

Other accounts of explanation include the following: Functional explanations—these explain social action in terms of the beneficial consequences that action has for the well-being or continuation of the larger social system. These explanations are quite common in ethnographic analysis. Materialist explanations—these explain human action (e.g., a social institution, political arrangement, particular social practice, group attitude, ideology, and so on) in terms of the relation of that action to the material environment or culture of a society or group (e.g., topography, climate, social arrangements, technological factors, and so on). Here are some examples: Banditry thrives in remote regions because the rugged terrain makes it difficult for the state to repress the practice; food taboos result from ecological crises; differences in the political attitudes among European workers result from the technical characteristics of different industrial systems and occupations. Materialist explanations incorporate the basic features of rational-choice or decision-theoretic explanations, which assume that individual behavior is goal directed and calculating and that social action can be explained as the aggregate consequence of the purposive actions of a large number of individuals. Although these three kinds of explanations differ from the covering-law model in the way they account for human action, all share the general goal of developing a causal explanation. There are varieties of qualitative methodologies in the social sciences that embrace this view of the general aim and nature of social theory. (See D. Little, *Varieties of Social Explanation,* Westview, 1991.)

<u>Explanation as the goal for the human sciences.</u> Defenders of *Verstehen approaches, phenomenological sociology, philosophical hermeneutics,* and *poststructuralism* strongly object to the idea that the human sciences should develop causal, lawlike theoretical explanations of *human action. Verstehen* and hermeneutic approaches argue that there is no place for such causal theories because human action can never be explained in this way; it can be interpreted only by developing an understanding of the meanings of particular social practices or actions. This interpretive understanding is provided by giving accounts of social action in terms of intersubjective meanings,

by exploring the various forms that meaningful social action assume (e.g., ritual, practice, rule following, drama, and so on), or through linguistic accounts showing how language is constitutive of reality (e.g., P. Winch, *The Idea of a Social Science and Its Relation to Philosophy*, Routledge and Kegan Paul, 1958; A. R. Louch, *Explanation and Human Action*, Univ. of California Press, 1969; C. Taylor, *Philosophical Papers, Vols. 1 and 2*, Cambridge Univ. Press, 1985). It is not uncommon for interpretivists to draw on insights from speech-act theory or the pragmatics (vs. the semantics) of language (e.g., J. L. Austin, H. P. Grice, J. Searle) that explore speech acts as intentional action. Phenomenological approaches to qualitative inquiry focus on describing and mapping the basic structures or features of lived experience rather than developing causal theories. Poststructural approaches mount a wide-ranging critique of not only causal explanatory theory but all forms of modern social theory as impossible and pointless in a postmodern world. They seek not to explain but to deconstruct human action and show the endless play of meanings involved therein. **See also CAUSAL ANALYSIS, THEORY.**

FALLIBILISM This is the doctrine that knowledge and beliefs are inherently uncertain, that scientific claims are always tentative. It received a good deal of attention in the writings of American pragmatists, most notably in the work of Charles Sanders Peirce (1839-1914) as part of his detailed critique of Cartesian epistemology. A fallibilistic attitude is also characteristic of the work of philosopher of science Karl Popper (1902-1994) who has argued that science progresses by means of a process of problem identification → tentative solutions (conjectures) → elimination of errors through the testing of conjectures (refutation) → further conjecture, and so on. Conjectures are always tentative, never certain, never beyond refutation. **See also PRAGMATISM.**

FEMINIST EPISTEMOLOGY There is no single feminist epistemology. Discussions of epistemology by feminists simultaneously exhibit a wide range of ideas including criticism of both traditional epistemology (*rationalism* and *empiricism*), arguments that reason and objectivity are gendered concepts, tension with *postmodernism,* and alliances with ideas of *critical social science* and *participatory action research.* Three strands of feminist epistemology have been identified, although there is great variance within each: (1) Feminist empiricism: A defense of experiential or observational data as the only legitimate basis for the testing of hypotheses and theory. Feminist empiricists argue that these kinds of data about women's experiences are traditionally missing from current medical, psychological, and sociological theory. They seek to rectify this situation by producing empirically more accurate pictures of social reality. Feminist empiricism does not accept without question, however, the methodological assumptions (e.g., detached objectivity, neutrality, and so forth) associated with empiricist epistemology. (2) Feminist standpoint epistemologies: Inquiry ought to begin in and be tested against the lived sociopolitical experiences of women, for women have a more complete and less distorted vision of real social relations unavailable to men insofar as they benefit from the exploitation of women. These epistemologies often draw on Marxist and neo-Marxist analyses of class domination and the division of labor in society. (3) Feminist *postmodernism:* This is a catch-all phrase for an incredibly rich variety of perspectives that in one sense 'come after' the first two epistemologies noted above. Postmodern epistemologies are in part characterized by debates between standpoint perspectives and defenders of *deconstructionism* and postmodern notions such as the suspicion of all universalizing claims, the rejection of truth as an oppressive illusion, and the relativizing of experience to local micropolitics. Some scholars see postmodernism and feminist theory as incompatible; others believe that insights of postmodernism—particularly its concerns with linking knowledge and power; its preoccupation with concrete, particular sites of struggles against oppression; its opening up of discourse to multiple voices; its critique of objectivity—actually serve to strengthen feminist epistemology. For more detail on these epistemologies and controversies, see Louise M. Antony and Charlotte Witt, eds., *A Mind of One's Own: Feminist Essays on Reason and Objectivity,* Westview, 1993; Sandra Harding, ed., *Feminism and Methodology,* Indiana Univ. Press, 1987;

Sandra Harding and Merrill B. Hintikka, eds., *Discovering Reality: Feminist Perspectives on Epistemology, Metaphysics, Methodology, and Philosophy of Science*, D. Reidel, 1983; Linda J. Nicholson, ed., *Feminism/Postmodernism*, Routledge, 1990. The relation between feminist epistemologies and the wide range of feminist methodologies is reviewed extensively in Mary Margaret Fonow and Judith A. Cook, eds., *Beyond Methodology: Feminist Scholarship as Lived Research*, Indiana Univ. Press, 1991, and Shulamit Reinharz, *Feminist Methods in Social Research*, Oxford Univ. Press, 1992. **See also** OBJECTIVE/OBJECTIVITY.

F

FIDELITY TO METHODOLOGICAL PRINCIPLES   See ETHNOGRAPHIC NATURALISM, THEORY.

FIDELITY TO PHENOMENON   See ETHNOGRAPHIC NATURALISM, THEORY.

FIELD   Traditionally, the field is the physical place where one goes to do *fieldwork*. For anthropologists this has often been some foreign land with arrival on site dutifully noted in what is called an arrival tale in the report of the fieldwork. More generally, it is where your colleagues say you are when you are doing your research: "Where's Mary?" "She's in the field." The notion of "field" as a place or situation where some particular *social action* transpires whether or not the inquirer is present sets the notion apart from the idea of an 'artificial' setting (i.e., a laboratory experiment) especially contrived by the inquirer. Thus the notion of the field is in part tied to the doctrine of *ethnographic naturalism*. The notion of what constitutes the field is presently under a great deal of reexamination. What once solely characterized what it meant to be in the field was being physically displaced from some comfortable familiar setting (i.e., the university) to some exotic, linguistically and physically challenging remote place. This traditional conception is undergoing revision as more and more fieldworkers undertake studies in nearby locales, including occasionally the fieldworker's own work setting. More significantly, the idea of a place 'out there' in which one studies is being challenged by arguments such as (1) "The field is not so much a place as it is a particular relation between oneself and others, involving a difficult combination of commitment and disengagement, relationship and separation" (R. Lederman, "Pretexts for Ethnography: On Reading Fieldnotes," in R. Sanjek, ed., *Fieldnotes*, Cornell Univ. Press, 1990, p. 88), and (2) "The 'field' is not an entity 'out there' that awaits discovery and exploration by the intrepid explorer. The field is not merely reported in the texts of fieldwork: It is constituted by our writing and reading" (P. Atkinson, *The Ethnographic Imagination*, Routledge, 1992, p. 8). **See also** FIELDWORK, PARTICIPANT OBSERVATION.

FIELD JOURNAL   A bound notebook that the fieldworker carries into the field and in which is recorded observational notes, personal notes, sketches, ideas, lists of terms, and so on. What exactly is contained in the field journal is a matter of individual style and need. **See also** FIELDNOTES.

FIELDNOTES   The common sense wisdom is that fieldnotes are data, but as the collection of essays edited by Roger Sanjek (*Fieldnotes*, Cornell Univ. Press, 1990) reveals, opinions vary widely on what fieldnotes are. Some fieldworkers define fieldnotes as 'raw' data or material—notes made in the field based on observations and conversations, rough diagrams and charts, lists of terms, and so on. Others contrast fieldnotes with data, defining fieldnotes more along the lines of daily entries made in a *field journal* to record thoughts, impressions, initial ideas, working hypotheses, issues to pursue, and so on. For some, fieldnotes include all those things collected in the course of *fieldwork*—the fieldwork journal, transcripts of conversations and interviews, photographs, audio- and videotapes, copies of documents, and artifacts. Others exclude some of these as not belonging to fieldnotes proper. Fieldnotes are very much prepared for an audience of one, the fieldworker, and thus are individualistic and personal and reflective of the unique ways individual fieldworkers conduct fieldwork. Common wisdom also holds that the written product of fieldwork—the ethnography, case study, and so forth—is based on fieldnotes. But that is only partially correct, for fieldworkers come back from the field with both fieldnotes (however defined) and 'headnotes'—the former written down, the latter continually evolving and changing. Written reports of fieldwork are a product of both (see S. Ottenberg, "Thirty Years of Fieldnotes: Changing Relationships to the Text" in the Sanjek collection).

Approaches to qualitative inquiry that place a premium on systematic, rigorous methods of generating and analyzing data will define fieldnotes as carefully prepared archives of data and documentation. Fieldnotes will be defined as the 'real' data and distinguished from headnotes and from a record of reactions or a chronology of ideas found in a fieldwork journal. Fieldnote data would be constructed on the analogy to data in the form of responses to a survey or the results of the application of a psychometric measure. 'Data' would be defined as tangible objects to be entered into files and records that can be manipulated and coded in various ways. (The logic of computer-assisted analysis of qualitative data seems to rest on this way of thinking about fieldnotes.) In sum, on a scientific conception of doing qualitative work, fieldwork → fieldnotes → written report of fieldwork are connected in something resembling a building-block model. Scientific analysis of qualitative data assumes that resulting interpretations or understandings of human action are capable of being found in or traced to discrete segments of data in the form of written notes on observations, typed transcripts, parts of documents, and so on. Yet, the definition of fieldnotes and their relationship to fieldwork activity and written reports of fieldwork is far more complex and problematic. Fieldnotes have a dynamic character (what one knows and records early on in fieldwork will be different than what one knows and records later) and preparing them requires interpretive and textualizing practices. **See also** ANALYZING QUALITATIVE DATA, THICK DESCRIPTION, FIELD, INSCRIPTION, TRANSCRIPTION.

FIELD RELATIONS   This is a shorthand way of referring to the complex set of logistical, procedural, ethical, and political dimensions of relating to informants, gatekeepers, respondents, and others in the *field* in which one studies. Included here are the responsibilities entailed in gaining access to settings, people, and documents; establishing and maintaining trust; negotiating a particular role in the setting; and departing the field (see, for example, W. B. Shaffir and R. A. Stebbins, eds., *Experiencing Fieldwork: An Inside View of Qualitative Research,* Sage, 1991; M. Punch, *The Politics and Ethics of Fieldwork,* Sage, 1986). Confessional tales included in fieldwork reports often focus on some aspect of field relations as well as on the trials and tribulations of fieldwork more generally (see J. VanMaanen, *Tales of the Field*, Univ. of Chicago Press, 1988). **See also** ETHICS OF QUALITATIVE INQUIRY, FIELDWORK, PARTICIPANT OBSERVATION.

FIELD STUDIES   A generic designation for all forms of social science research (e.g., *case study research, ethnography,* and so on) that involve direct, first-hand observation in naturally occurring situations or events and that rely principally on techniques of *participant observation* and *interviewing.* Field studies can involve the generation of both numeric and nonnumeric data. See John Lofland and Lyn H. Lofland, *Analyzing Social Settings,* 3rd ed., Wadsworth, 1995, for a guide to the primary activities of assembling data, focusing the data, and analyzing data that are entailed in all such studies. Not all qualitative studies are necessarily field studies, for a qualitative inquirer could use existing texts, documents, or cultural artifacts as the data for analysis. **See also** FIELD, FIELDWORK.

FIELDWORK   This term refers to all those activities that one engages in while in the *field,* including watching, listening, conversing, recording, interpreting, dealing with logistics, facing ethical and political dilemmas, and so on. It is an intensely personal and social process requiring both physical and intellectual stamina, political acumen, and moral sensitivity. *Participant observation* has traditionally been thought of as the *methodology* employed in fieldwork, but interview studies (including life history work, oral history, and so on), case studies of various kinds, and coparticipative inquiries like *action research* all entail some aspects of fieldwork as well. In the literature, the fieldwork process is often reconstructed into phases (e.g., gaining entry, negotiating access, maintaining *field relations,* collecting and analyzing data, exiting the field) to address in some manageable way all the various skills, knowledge, and attitudes entangled in fieldwork activity. Yet, in actual practice, fieldwork rarely unfolds in any neatly linear fashion.

Fieldwork is often discussed more as a set of tool skills rather than a way of being-in-the-world in relation to others. This is due, in part, to connotations associated with the term "field<u>work</u>" coupled with the lingering legacy of *logical empiricism* that stresses the importance of *method* in defining scientific inquiry. In other words, fieldwork is traditionally defined as a particular kind of labor or work one engages in to produce results. This labor requires means-end knowledge, a set of procedural or tool skills (a kind of technical knowledge) used to solve the puzzle of understanding human action. This is not to deny that there is extensive literature on field relations and fieldwork ethics. But this literature is also often presented as a tool-like knowledge—a set of guidelines, procedures, and obligations entailed in the epistemologically responsible and ethically correct use of data-gathering and analysis tools. The notion of fieldwork as a tool skill set seems to be particularly prominent in the applied fields for whom the discovery of qualitative inquiry is more recent (e.g., health professions, social services administration, education, journalism, telecommunications).

F

A refiguration of what fieldwork is and what fieldwork knowledge consists of, however, is at least suggested in ideas from *social constructionism, pragmatism, critical social science,* and *philosophical hermeneutics.* This refiguration does not mean abandoning notions of technical competence in skills of watching, listening, conversing, and recording. Nor does it deny the need for familiarity with ethical principles. Rather, the shift in thinking about fieldwork means resetting those concerns within a different framework for knowledge and a different mode of the inquirer's engagement with the social world. When fieldwork is defined as *praxis* requiring a kind of *practical-moral knowledge,* emphasis shifts from a 'tool skill set' to exploring the following ideas: the fieldworker's way of being-in-the world; the difference between wisdom and knowledge; the moral and personal commitments to dialogue that fieldwork entails; the kind of knowledge of other people it requires; the incoherence, ambiguity, and contradictoriness of experience; and fieldwork as a kind of communicative action or practical discourse. **See also** ETHICS OF QUALITATIVE INQUIRY, PARTICIPANT OBSERVATION.

FOUNDATIONALIST EPISTEMOLOGY See NONFOUNDATIONAL EPISTEMOLOGY, OBJECTIVISM.

FRANKFURT SCHOOL The name given to members of the Marxist-oriented *Institut für Sozialforschung* (Institute for Social Research) founded in 1923 in Frankfurt, Germany. Because most of the institute's members were Marxists and Jews, the institute was forced into exile by the Nazis. In 1934, it formally moved to Columbia University. In this institute, a blend of explanatory social research, normative critique, and philosophical reflection divorced from orthodox Marxism emerged that came to be called a 'critical theory' of society by its members in the mid-1930s. Its most influential director was Max Horkheimer (1895-1973) and its first generation included the social theorists T. W. Adorno (1903-1969), Herbert Marcuse (1898-1979), Walter Benjamin (1892-1940), and Erich Fromm (1900-1980), among others. Jürgen Habermas, a student of both Adorno and Horkheimer, is perhaps the most widely known member of the second generation of critical theorists to emerge from the institute after its return to Germany in 1950. **See also** CRITICAL SOCIAL SCIENCE.

FUNCTIONALISM   Functionalist theories or models aim to explain human behavior (e.g., rituals, customs, ceremonies) and social-cultural institutions (e.g., family, church, state) in terms of the functions they perform in a particular group, society, culture, or community. In sociology, the source of functionalism is most often associated with the work of Emile Durkheim (1858-1917) and in anthropology with the work of Bronislaw Malinowski (1884-1942). A variation called structural functionalism was developed by the anthropologist Alfred Radcliffe-Brown (1881-1995), who distinguished between structure (a network of social relations and institutions comprising the permanent framework of society) and function (the way in which these relations and institutions contributed to the stable functioning of society). Functionalist explanations are also found in political science and systems theory. A common criticism of these kinds of explanations is that they assume stability and harmonious function of aspects of a society or culture and thus fail to address conflict. **See also** EXPLANATION.

GEISTESWISSENSCHAFT A German term usually translated as "human sciences." **See** SCIENCE, *VERSTEHEN*.

GENERALIZATION A general statement or proposition made by drawing an inference from observation of the particular. Generalization is an act of reasoning from the observed to the unobserved, from a specific instance to all instances believed to be like the instance in question. Theories are generalizations; they explain some phenomenon across a variety of specific instances or cases of that phenomenon. Generalization, or generalizability (also called external validity), is traditionally held to be one of the *criteria* for social scientific inquiry. In qualitative inquiry, four different positions on the issue of generalization are discernible: (1) Some radical postmodernists repudiate any and all attempts to generalize. They are opposed to *theory* of any kind and look instead to the uniqueness of events and perspectives. They take an antitheoretical and antigeneralizing interest in the contingent and specific circumstances of everyday life events; they emphasize local narratives, local knowledge. (2) A less radical and more affirmative postmodern approach to generalizing is explained by Norman Denzin (*Interpretive Interactionism*, Sage, 1989). He builds a case for the study of biographies and lived experiences that issues in texts that are at once contextual, multivoiced, interactional, and interpretive. These texts contribute to theoretical understanding by illuminating interpretive theories already at work in the connections that frame the stories that are told. The inquirer engages in generalizing by making vivid and critically examining the connections between unique, uncommon lived experiences and the commonality of groups, social relationships, and culturally constructed images that partially define those experiences. (3) Other qualitative inquirers share the emphasis on the importance of understanding the specific, the local, the particular, but seek to reconcile this with the idea of generalization by arguing for extrapolation or *transferability* of findings from a specific *case*. Extrapolation is achieved in one of two ways: by *analytic generalization* or by case-to-case transfer. In the former, the inquirer uses findings from a specific case to test, refine, or modify some theory or theoretical idea, concept, or model. Clifford Geertz (see "Thick Description: Toward an Interpretive Theory of Culture," in Geertz, *The Interpretation of Cultures*, Basic Books, 1983), for example, argues that ethnography always is microscopic or situation specific. "The important thing about the anthropologist's findings," he says, "is their complex specificness, their circumstantiality." Yet specific cases provide the context-specific stuff or material that makes it possible to think "realistically and concretely about" social scientific concepts and theories (e.g., modernization, stratification, legitimacy, integration, conflict, charisma, structure, and so on) and to work "creatively and imaginatively with them." (See also M. Burawoy et al., *Ethnography Unbound: Power and Resistance in the Modern Metropolis*, Univ. of California Press, 1992.) Case-to-case transfer is a different kind of extrapolation. For example, Yvonna Lincoln and Egon Guba (*Naturalistic Inquiry*, Sage, 1985) urge the investigator to provide sufficient detail about the circumstances of the situation or case that was studied so readers can engage in reasonable but modest speculation about whether findings are applicable to other cases with similar circumstances. Both transferability and analytic generalization are ways to deal with the apparent paradox of qualitative work: its avowed focus on the particular and its simultaneous interest in the general. (4) Still other qualitative inquirers emphasize that qualitative work produces a kind of knowledge that is fundamentally different from the kind of knowledge represented in generalizations. They argue that qualitative studies yield knowledge of particulars, a kind of practical knowledge that Aristotle called *phronesis*. It is characterized by qualities of concreteness, attention to the contingent features of the case at hand, temporality, and openness to doubt. This kind of knowledge stands in contrast to theoretical knowledge or scientific understanding (what Aristotle called *episteme*), which is expressed in general propositions (e.g., rules, laws, principles, theories). Scientific understanding is characterized by qualities of abstractness or idealization, atemporality or timelessness, and necessity. *Phronesis* and *episteme* are essentially different types of knowledge. Both kinds of knowledge may be necessary to understand the world, but the former cannot be reduced to the latter.

One's understanding of the meaning and importance of generalization affects one's view of the 'use' of qualitative studies. Inquirers committed to the view that qualitative studies yield practical knowledge take exception to the traditional understanding of why we engage in the study of particulars and how we use such knowledge. The traditional conception is that the aim of social inquiry (whether qualitative or quantitative) is to develop empirical, explanatory **theory**. Particular cases are studied for the purpose of forming general theoretical knowledge; they are not interesting in their own right. Once we are in possession of theory we can, over time, achieve intellectual and practical mastery of the social world (in much the same manner that possessing a body of empirical explanatory theory in the natural sciences facilitates mastery of the physical world). A particular relationship between theory and practice or action is assumed here: The way to change the social circumstances of education, health care, work life, and so forth is through the technical application of social scientific knowledge (especially knowledge of the probable consequences of different courses of action) to social problems. But defenders of qualitative work as contributing to *phronesis* argue that we study the particular for a completely different reason. The study of the particular helps train perception and increase the capacity for practical reasoning and deliberation in those many situations in life that are full of too many details, idiosyncrasies, and exceptional aspects to permit the application of general knowledge. In sum, on this conception of the use of qualitative studies, the aim is to study specific cases—not to develop or elaborate on general theoretical knowledge, but to make it possible to develop powers of perception and thereby enhance practical wisdom. **See also** INFERENCE, PRAXIS.

GENERATING DATA   It is a common mistake to think that data are somehow discovered and collected (i.e., gathered), like picking berries from the vine. On the contrary, what constitutes data depends on one's inquiry purposes and the questions one seeks to answer. Data are generated or constructed by various means that are deemed appropriate to serving those purposes and answering those questions.

GROUNDED THEORY METHODOLOGY   The term "grounded theory" is often used in a nonspecific way to refer to any approach to developing theoretical ideas (concepts, models, formal theories) that somehow begins with data. But grounded theory methodology is a specific, highly developed, rigorous set of procedures for producing substantive theory of social phenomena. This approach to the analysis of qualitative data simultaneously employs techniques of induction, deduction, and verification to develop theory. Experience with data generates insights, hypotheses, and generative questions, which are pursued through further data collection. As tentative answers to questions are developed and concepts are constructed, these constructions are verified through further data collection. Grounded theory methodology requires a concept-indicator model of analysis, which, in turn, employs the method of constant comparison. Empirical indicators from the data (actions and events observed, recorded, or described in documents in the words of interviewees and respondents) are looked at for similarities and differences. From this process the analyst identifies underlying uniformities in the indicators and produces a coded category or concept. Concepts are compared with more empirical indicators and with each other to sharpen the definition of the concept and to define its properties. Theories are formed from proposing plausible relationships among concepts and sets of concepts. Tentative theories or theoretical propositions are further explored through additional instances of data. The testing of the emergent theory is guided by theoretical sampling. Theoretical sampling means that the sampling of additional incidents, events, activities, populations, and so on is directed by the evolving theoretical constructs. Comparisons between the explanatory adequacy of the theoretical constructs and these additional empirical indicators go on continuously until theoretical saturation is reached (i.e., additional analysis no longer contributes to anything new about a concept). In this way, the resulting theory is considered conceptually dense and grounded in the data. See B. Glaser and A. Strauss, *The Discovery of Grounded Theory*, Aldine, 1967, and *Awareness of Dying*, Aldine, 1965; A. Strauss, *Qualitative Analysis for Social Scientists*, Cambridge Univ. Press, 1987; A. Strauss and J. Corbin, *Basics of Qualitative Research: Grounded Theory Procedures and Techniques*, Sage, 1990. For a criticism of this approach to developing sociological theory, see M. Burawoy et al., *Ethnography Unbound: Power and Resistance in the Modern Metropolis*, Univ. of California Press, 1992. **See also** THEORY.

G

HERMENEUTICS This term generally refers to the art, theory, and philosophy of the interpretation of meaning of an object (a *text,* a work of art, *human action,* the utterances of another speaker, and so on). There is, however, a variety of definitions of hermeneutics behind which lay complex theoretical disputes. Friedrich Schleiermacher (1768-1834), who is generally recognized as a creator of modern hermeneutic theory, defined hermeneutics as the art of understanding practiced in reading classical, biblical, and legal texts. At the beginning of the twentieth century, Wilhelm Dilthey (1833-1911) extended the idea of hermeneutics to the epistemology and methodology of the human sciences. From Dilthey onward to the contemporary human sciences, hermeneutics has meant the theory of interpretation as a particular methodology. Yet, this interpretation was challenged by Martin Heidegger (1889-1976), who understood hermeneutics to be the existential-phenomenological analysis of the constitution of *Dasein* ('existence' or 'Being-in-the-world'). He argued that hermeneutics ('understanding') is a fundamental concept of *ontology,* that is, a basic characteristic of human existence. Hans-Georg Gadamer developed Heidegger's ideas of hermeneutics (or 'understanding') as a primary and universal way of our being in the world and argued for hermeneutics as a kind of practical philosophy. Furthermore, because understanding is viewed as a linguistic event, Gadamer explored the centrality of language and dialogue to understanding. For overviews of different hermeneutic theories see Josef Bleicher, *Contemporary Hermeneutics: Hermeneutics as Method, Philosophy, and Critique,* Routledge and Kegan Paul, 1980. The importance of hermeneutics for the human sciences in general and qualitative inquiry in particular is marked by the debates that have unfolded among defenders of conservative or objectivist hermeneutics, philosophical hermeneutics, and radical hermeneutics or deconstructionism. Along with *Verstehende Sociology,* the German tradition of hermeneutical thought serves as the major source of ideas for qualitative inquiry. **See also** CRITICAL HERMENEUTICS, DECONSTRUCTIONISM, HERMENEUTICS OF SUSPICION, PHILOSOPHICAL HERMENEUTICS, TEXT, VALIDATION HERMENEUTICS.

HERMENEUTIC CIRCLE   There are two senses of this term. In the simplest sense, the hermeneutic circle refers to relation of parts of a *text* to the whole text: The interpretation of each part depends on the interpretation of the whole and vice-versa. On a more sophisticated definition, the hermeneutic circle is an ontological condition of understanding. In other words, it points to the fact that being an interpreter is an inescapable condition of what it means to be human. The image of a circle refers to the fact that the interpreter is bound to a general communal tradition on one hand and to the particular object of interpretation on the other. The notion is best captured in the following figure taken from S. Gallagher, *Hermeneutics and Education,* SUNY Press, 1992, p. 106).

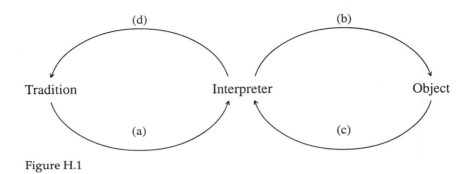

Figure H.1

Gallagher explains that the anterior operation of tradition (a) as a fore-structure of understanding both conditions and suggests the fore-conceptions (b) that the inquirer brings to interpret the object (a text or another human being). The feedback from the reading of the text (or from another human being's response in a conversation) motivates a new projection of meaning (interpretation). The relations (b) and (c) represent the hermeneutic circle; (d) indicates that in the process of interpreting, the inquirer's relation to a particular tradition can change; fore-conceptions can be challenged and modified, and so on. The fact that there is no escaping the hermeneutic circle reveals its ontological character, that is, we are 'interpretive' beings.

This notion of a hermeneutic circle points to the circularity of interpretation in a strong sense: Every interpretation is itself based on another interpretation. For the defender of this ontological conception of hermeneutics there are no brute data (see *empiricism*) that somehow lie 'outside' of interpretation. For an explanation of this idea—that is, that there is no 'final' interpretation and that one can only appeal to interpretations of interpretations—see Charles Taylor, "Interpretation and the Sciences of Man," originally in *Review of Metaphysics*, 1971, 25: 3-51. **See also** HERMENEUTICS.

HERMENEUTICS OF SUSPICION   A term coined by Paul Ricoeur to characterize the hermeneutical philosophy of the more radical followers of Nietzsche, principally Derrida and Foucault (1926-1984).

(See, for example, John Caputo, *Radical Hermeneutics: Repetition, Deconstruction, and the Hermeneutic Project,* Indiana Univ. Press, 1987.) Also called radical or deconstructionist hermeneutics, this philosophy is profoundly suspicious of whatever purports to be the truth; it argues that all interpretations are false and there is no escape from false consciousness. Shaun Gallagher (*Hermeneutics and Education,* SUNY Press, 1992, p. 21) provides this brief characterization: "The task of the hermeneutics of suspicion is to decipher, decode, or unmask the 'reality' or 'truth' of consciousness, capitalism, and Christian (= Western) metaphysics to show the contingency and relativity of these systems." Habermas' hermeneutic philosophy belongs to this view to the extent that it seeks to unmask false consciousness. Yet, because Habermas trusts in language and dialogue and holds out hope for the restoration of meaning and institutions, he also shares something with the hermeneutic philosophy of Gadamer and what is called the hermeneutics of trust. See also **DECONSTRUCTIONISM, PHILOSOPHICAL HERMENEUTICS.**

HOLISM   See **REDUCTIONISM.**

HUMAN ACTION   Qualitative inquirers often refer to the object of study as that of meaningful human or social 'action' as opposed to human or social 'behavior.' This language, in part, reflects a distinction between meaningful action and merely reactive behavior introduced by Max Weber (1864-1920) and elaborated by symbolic interactionists like George Herbert Mead (1863-1931). The emphasis on action reflects two important ideas: First, that the acting individual attaches subjective meaning to her or his behavior; in other words, it is a purposive, intentional, goal-directed act, not a simple observable physical response to a stimulus (as claimed, for example, in *behaviorism*). Second, that understanding subjective meaning requires understanding not simply individual beliefs, attitudes, motives, intentions, values, and the like but intersubjective or shared meanings, values, understandings, and so on that interpenetrate individual thought and action. Thus, the qualitative inquirer assumes that subjectivity is not a matter of individual psychological attributes, but is constituted intersubjectively. In his frequently cited essay, "Interpretation and the Sciences of Man" (originally appearing in the *Review of Metaphysics,* 1971, 25: 3-51), Charles Taylor discusses this notion of intersubjective meaning. Taylor argues that a strict neobehaviorist, empiricist account that claims human behavior can be explained simply by linking actors' physically observable behaviors to an inventory of individual actors' attitudes, beliefs, and other psychological states is mistaken. In Taylor's view, this completely overlooks the notion of intersubjective, shared meanings.

Weber's discussion of meaning and social action is found in his essay "Basic Sociological Terms," in *Economy and Society*, G. Roth and C. Wittich, eds., Bedminster, 1968. It was here that he also introduced the idea that social action can be oriented in different ways, including an instrumentally rational (*zweckrational*) orientation. In the work of Jürgen Habermas (*The Theory of Communicative Action, Vol. 1—Reason and Rationalization of Society*, trans. T. McCarthy, Beacon, 1981), a sharp critique of strategic, instrumental, or purposive-rational social action figures prominently. Habermas builds a case for communicative human action grounded in an emancipatory cognitive *interest* (vs. *zweckrational* grounded in a technical, instrumental, cognitive interest). This work forms the basis of some qualitative methodologies that are influenced by critical theory. **See also** INTEREST, LIFEWORLD, UNDERSTANDING, *VERSTEHEN*.

HYPOTHETICO-DEDUCTIVE METHOD   The covering-law model of *explanation* holds that human behavior is explained when the inquirer has discovered the relevant generalizations that 'cover' the case to be explained. This model of explanation uses the hypothetico-deductive method to form hypotheses, deduce implications, and to test those hypotheses against experience. The steps in the ideal version of the method are the following: (1) Theory provides the definitions, assumptions, and hypotheses about human behavior from which (2) predictions about behavior are logically deduced. (3) Those predictions are then tested through a process of empirical observation. (4) From the results of observations, the inquirer concludes either that the theory appears consistent with the facts (i.e., it explains the behavior) or the theory is inconsistent with the facts. (5) If it is consistent, no further work is needed. If it is inconsistent, then the theory must be either discarded in favor of a better theory or modified to accommodate the newly required facts. See Martin Hollis, *The Philosophy of Social Science*, Cambridge Univ. Press, 1994, esp. Chap. 3.

I

IDEALISM Idealist explanations of sociocultural and historical phenomena give priority to mental phenomena, and thus contrast with materialist explanations that give primacy to material/physical phenomena and processes. This philosophical doctrine holds that the world (reality, real objects) does not exist independently of minds. Thus it stands in opposition both to *realism,* which defines the world (objects of knowledge) as a real structure that exists independently of our experience with it, our knowledge of it, and the conditions that allow us access to it, and to strict or direct *empiricism,* which claims the objects of knowledge are simply observable atomistic events (see, for example, R. Bhaskar, *A Realist Theory of Science,* 2nd ed., Harvester, 1978). An idealist does not necessarily hold that the natural and social worlds are unreal or nonexistent, but that there is no unmediated access to such worlds, that is, no 'direct' understanding of the world. The world is always interpreted through mind. As is the case with any philosophical notion with a long history, idealism is a complicated view with many varieties. It is a philosophy that tries to say something about what lies behind or beyond experience and in that sense early nineteenth-century German idealism (J. G. Fichte [1762-1814], F. W. J. Schelling [1775-1854], G. W. F. Hegel [1770-1831], all building on Immanuel Kant's [1724-1804] transcendental idealism) served as the fertile ground for the late nineteenth- and early twentieth-century reaction to *logical positivism's* insistence on a strict empiricism. The spirit of idealism, its recognition of the importance of mind, life, emotion, and so forth, is the well-spring of qualitative work although not all so-called qualitative inquirers are necessarily philosophical idealists. **See also** RE-ALISM.

I

IDEOLOGY   Although the term has been employed in many ways, one common usage is to refer to a set of social, political, and moral values, attitudes, outlooks, and beliefs that shape a social group's interpretation of its behavior and its world. Following a usage established by Karl Marx (1818-1883), to label an outlook as 'ideological' typically is to criticize it for obscuring or distorting the truth. In a logical empiricist interpretation of social science, empirical explanatory social theories are said to be (or ought to be) free of ideological bias and hence neutral or objective. But a number of scholars have argued that social inquiry is inevitably ideological in the sense that it is based on hidden value biases (see, for example, R. J. Bernstein, *The Restructuring of Social and Political Theory*, Univ. of Pennsylvania Press, 1976; M. Root, *Philosophy of Social Science*, Blackwell, 1993; C. Taylor, *Philosophical Papers, Vol. 2*, Cambridge Univ. Press, 1985). The feminist and Marxist scholar Dorothy Smith (*The Conceptual Practices of Power*, Northeastern Univ. Press, 1990, pp. 42-43) advocates ideology-critique as a method of social inquiry. She claims that "ideological practices ensure that the determinations of our everyday, experienced world remain mysterious by preventing us from making them problems for inquiry." She urges social inquirers to think ideologically by which she means "to think in situationally determined modes since ideology deprives us of access to, hence critique of, the social relational substructure of our experience." For an instructive review of various uses of the term, as well as the notion of ideology-critique, see Nicholas C. Burbules, "Forms of Ideology-Critique: A Pedagogical Perspective," in P. L. McLaren and J. M. Giarelli, eds., *Critical Theory and Educational Research*, SUNY Press, 1995.

IDIOGRAPHIC KNOWLEDGE   See *VERSTEHEN*.

INDEXICAL MEANING (OR EXPRESSION)   Many versions of qualitative inquiry assume that our use of written or spoken language is indexical, which means that the meaning of language is dependent on the context of its use and hence language conveys more than can be said (or written) in the words alone. It is in light of this assumption that Clifford Geertz's oft-quoted explanation of interpretive inquiry makes sense (see his essay "Thick Description: Toward an Interpretive Theory of Culture," reprinted in Geertz, *The Interpretation of Cultures*, Basic Books, 1973). Geertz argued that the ethnographer "inscribes" (writes down) social discourse, but that what he or she writes down is not the event of speaking itself (i.e., the language and actions that comprise the discourse) but the "said" of speaking—the meaning of the event, not the event as event.

The notion of indexical meanings or expressions challenges the idea that the interpretive inquirer merely represents what he or she hears and sees—that is, simply observes and records speech and action. If meanings of speech and action are indexical, then the interpreter must somehow come to understand and eventually portray the context in which meanings are situated. Writing about that context, about situated use, or about what Geertz refers to as the thought, gist, or content of speaking and acting is an act of interpretation, not mere representation. **See also ETHNOMETHODOLOGY, INSCRIPTION, REPRESENTATION, THICK DESCRIPTION.**

INDUCTIVE ANALYSIS   A common refrain heard in qualitative studies is that they are distinguishable by their commitment to inductive analysis, which usually is defined as working from the data of specific cases to a more general conclusion. But this understanding of inductive analysis is by no means unique to qualitative work; much of probability theory and statistics is part of this logic of induction. There is something of a half-truth in the claim that qualitative studies are inductive. Qualitative analysis often does indeed begin with the data of specific cases, but that simply means that its efforts at analysis are grounded in data and <u>not speculative or abstract.</u> Qualitative analysis often (but not always) seeks to construct hypotheses by mucking around for ideas and hunches in the data rather than deriving those hypotheses in the first instance from established theory. But that is not an approach unique to qualitative studies, nor is it a good definition of inductive inference. Analysis in qualitative studies typically involves all forms of inference, including induction, deduction, and abduction. The claim that qualitative studies are 'inductive' may actually be a way of saying that they reject the *hypothetico-deductive* method of explanation in the social sciences. **See also** EXPLANATION, INFERENCE.

INDUCTIVE-STATISTICAL EXPLANATION   See EXPLANATION.

INFERENCE   To make an inference is to draw a conclusion from particular premises. Three kinds of rules or procedures for making inferences are deductive, inductive, and abductive. In deduction, the conclusion <u>must</u> follow from the premises (in other words, it is logically impossible for the conclusion to be false if the premises are true). A common legitimate principle of deductive inference (or legitimate deductive argument) employed in social science is modus tollens, which takes the following form:

	Modus Tollens
Premise 1:	If p then q
Premise 2:	Not q
Inference:	Therefore, not p.

Inductive inferences (and arguments) are more typical in social scientific inquiry. One kind of inductive inference relies on the principle of enumeration to reach a general conclusion about a group or class of individuals or events from observations of a specific set of individuals or events. The inference-making process is something like this: I have observed a suitable number of As under a reasonably wide variety of circumstances and have seen that they are Bs; hence, I infer that <u>all</u> As are Bs. In other words, I generalize the conclusion derived from my sample of As to all As. (Of course, the potential threat to the integrity of the inference here is how to determine what constitutes a suitable number of observations and a reasonably wide variety of circumstances.) A second kind of inductive inference is a statistical argument, which also depends on the principle of enumeration but in which the conclusion is stated in probabilistic terms such as "most," "many," "rarely," "some," and so on rather than "all" or "always."

An abductive inference (or abductive reasoning) is also called an inference to the best explanation. Imagine that you are examining a set of evidence and have devised a number of possible hypotheses that might explain the evidence. Inference to the best explanation is selecting that one hypothesis that provides the best explanation of the available evidence. The kind of inference making that takes place here assumes that inquiry is a kind of puzzle that requires speculation and best guesses. Abductive inference is explained by C. S. Peirce (1839-1914) but it also bears some similarity to Karl Popper's (1902-1994) conception of science as a process of conjectures and refutations. **See also** GENERALIZATION.

INFORMANT   See KEY INFORMANT.

INSCRIPTION   Literally, this term means to "write down," but its connotations in contemporary fieldwork are more profound and suggest that "writing down" is not so simple an act. Clifford Geertz was among the first to challenge the idea that a fieldworker merely observes and records. He argued that the correct answer to the question "What does the ethnographer do?" is "He or she writes." Yet, postmodern ethnography challenges the centrality of inscription as the origin of realistic description in fieldwork (see, for example, J. Clifford, "Notes on (Field)notes" in R. Sanjek, ed., *Fieldnotes*, Cornell Univ. Press, 1990). Inscription signals that writing down (and this includes photographing, videotaping, or audiotaping) is far from mere mechanical recording. The act of writing requires prior focus, selection, and interpretation. Furthermore, inscription signals an interruption in the fieldworker's attention to the flow of social discourse (speech and action). The fieldworker as participant observer turns away from that discourse to make a note (mental or written, long fieldnote, or scratch note). Hence, inscription is not some orderly process of data 'collection' or 'gathering' but an act of selective attention; a particular kind of practice whereby data are generated, undertaken in the midst of other activity. **See also** FIELD-NOTES, REPRESENTATION, THICK DESCRIPTION, TRANSCRIPTION.

INSIDER/OUTSIDER PERSPECTIVE   This is one way of thinking about the difference in the *epistemologies* of *hermeneutics* and *naturalism* or the difference between *understanding* and *explanation.* An internalist or insider perspective holds that knowledge of the social world must start from the insider or social actor's account of what social life means. To 'know' the world of *human action* is to 'understand' the subjective meanings of that action to the actors. In contrast, an externalist or outsider perspective argues that knowledge of the social world consists in causal explanations of human behavior. The social world (much like the natural world) can be viewed with a spectator's detachment. In fact, this kind of 'outside' objective stance is necessary to develop explanations (much like the explanations fashioned in the natural sciences) that are grounded in either sensory observations (*logical positivism*) or underlying causes, mechanisms, necessities, and so on (scientific *realism*).

INSTRUMENTALISM   At least two senses of this term are important for understanding something of the foundations of qualitative inquiry. (1) The *logical positivists* held an instrumentalist view of theories and theoretical terms. They were not concerned with whether scientific theories actually explained the 'real' world. Rather, theories and concepts were nothing more than tools, devices, or instruments allowing scientists to move from a set of observation statements to another set of predicted observations. In this sense, logical positivists privileged observation statements over theoretical terms or reduced the latter to the former. (2) The term "instrumentalism" or "instrumental rationality" also figures prominently in the critique of empirical-analytic sciences by critical theorists, postmodernists, poststructuralists, feminists, and others. Here the term means something like means-end thinking. The argument is that empirical-analytic sciences serve an interest in the prediction and instrumental control of nature. When this idea is extended to the social or human sciences, it results in the manipulation of social relations, the elevation of technical means over moral purposes, the support of dominant political and social classes, and the impoverishment of democratic political discussion (see, for example, B. Fay,

Social Theory and Political Practice, Holmes and Meier, 1976). **See also** REALISM.

INTEREST   This notion plays an important role in Jürgen Habermas' critical theory of society (*Knowledge and Human Interests,* trans. J. J. Shapiro, Beacon, 1971). The term "interests" for Habermas does not mean individual preferences but rather cognitive or knowledge-constitutive ideas, which means they determine what counts as knowledge. These interests are also defined as basic or fundamental, meaning they are not just part of an *epistemology* or way of knowing the world, but rooted in human nature or particular aspects of social life. Habermas described three primary cognitive interests—technical, practical, and emancipatory—and identified each with a different form of social science. The technical interest requires the isolation of objects and events to examine them empirically and form theoretical explanations of them. The empirical-analytic disciplines are informed by this technical interest as well as by a conception of social life as purposive-rational or instrumental action (or simply "work," i.e., the ways in which we manipulate and control our world to survive and thrive in it). *Nomological* knowledge is essential to this conception. The practical interest is concerned with developing intersubjective understanding and agreement on values, meanings, and practices. The historical-hermeneutic disciplines are guided by this interest as well as by the assumption that human life is characterized by interaction or communicative action through which we establish consensual norms for behavior and mutual understanding of intentions and obligations. The emancipatory interest defines the bid to provide an account of the genesis of meanings, values, and practices and how they are reflections of changing social structures. Critically oriented social sciences are grounded in this interest as well as in the assumption that reflection is central to social life. Reflection requires free, open communication as well as the material conditions that permit this kind of communication to determine how our meanings, practices, and values may be ideologically frozen or distorted. Habermas regarded the emancipatory interest as the most basic interest. **See also CRITICAL SOCIAL SCIENCE.**

INTERPRETATION   A clarification, explication, or explanation of the meaning of some phenomenon. The claims of both the natural and human or social sciences are interpretations in this sense. "Interpretation" is often used, however, to signal a difference between the two sciences: The natural sciences 'explain' the behavior of natural phenomena in terms of causes; the human sciences 'interpret' or 'understand' the meaning of *social action*. Here interpretation is used as a synonym for *hermeneutics* or *Verstehen*.

INTERSUBJECTIVITY (INTERSUBJECTIVE)   Literally, this means occurring between or among (or accessible to) two or more separate subjects or conscious minds. It is one way of defining objectivity. For many qualitative inquirers, however, the term signals the character or nature of the *life-world*. The everyday life-world is made up of our individual interpretations of experience, behavior, action, meaning, and so forth. Yet these interpretations are not simply subjective (i.e., the perspectives of individual subjects), and we could not understand shared or common interpretations by somehow summing up or averaging the interpretations of all subjects. Our interpretive schemes, our ways of making meaning of experience, are essentially social or intersubjective. Hence, intersubjectivity lies at the heart of subjectivity. **See also** LIFE-WORLD, HUMAN ACTION, *VERSTEHEN*.

INTERVIEWING   There are at least three ways to examine interviewing within qualitative studies: (1) The first way is as a set of techniques for generating and analyzing data from structured, group, and unstructured interviews with *respondents*, participants, and *key informants*. Concerns here include the logistics and mechanics of arranging and conducting interviews, and the costs and benefits of various interview strategies. Generally, qualitative studies make greatest use of unstructured, open-ended, informal interviews for they allow the most flexibility and responsiveness to emerging issues for both respondents and interviewees. But the use of structured open- (and closed-) ended interviews is not uncommon in field studies where time is limited, where it is desirable to get some specific or focused information from a large number of people, or both. (2) The second is as a particular kind of human encounter in the *field* that entails special ethical considerations concerning confidentiality, anonymity, and so on. Concerns here include obtaining informed consent, dealing with sensitive information, and so on.

(3) And last, as a linguistic event unfolding in particular sociopolitical contexts. This is often difficult to grasp because the tendency is to conceptualize interviewing in the language of survey research. Elliot Mishler (*Research Interviewing: Context and Narrative,* Harvard Univ. Press, 1986) explains that interviewing in survey research rests on three assumptions: (1) the interview is a behavioral event; it is spoken of as "verbal behavior," a "verbal exchange," or "pattern of verbal interaction"; (2) the interview process is framed within the context of stimulus-response (question and answer); (3) the interview situation is isolated from cultural and situational norms and frameworks of meaning. In contrast, it has become increasingly common in qualitative studies to view the interview as a form of discourse between two or more speakers or as a linguistic event in which the meanings of questions and responses are contextually grounded and jointly constructed by interviewer and respondent. This framework for interviewing (in contrast to the traditional survey research paradigm) introduces a variety of new considerations about how the interview event is constructed. Feminist interview research (see, for example, S. Reinharz, *Feminist Methods in Social Research,* Oxford Univ. Press, 1992, Chap. 2), for example, explores issues such as the consequences of close versus distant relations with interviewees, hierarchical researcher-respondent relationships, believing and being trusted, advocacy, and self-disclosure that are attendant on the particular circumstances in which open-ended, in-depth interviews are used. **See also** LIFE-HISTORY METHODOLOGY, TRANSCRIPTION.

I

JUDGMENT   A considered, deliberate opinion based on good reasons. Benjamin Barber (*The Conquest of Politics*, Princeton Univ. Press, 1988, p. 194) argues that judgment "entails more than mere observation, but it falls short of full nomothetic explanation. . . . Less subjective than the expression of rank personal prejudice, it is nonetheless less objective than the claim to scientific or metaphysical truth. It occupies precisely the ambiguous realm that lies between opinion and certainty." The elimination of fallible human judgment (or interpretation) in the testing of scientific hypotheses was a goal of *logical positivism* and *logical empiricism.* This philosophy assumed that logical rules could be established for linking observational statements to theoretical terms and that logical rules could govern the formation of a scientific *explanation.* These rules could be applied algorithmically, eliminating the need for human interpretation. The distinction drawn by logical empiricists between the context of discovery and the context of justification reflected this concern. The context of discovery referred to the process by which a scientist happened to think up a scientific theory or hypothesis. Here the psychology of human judgment was clearly involved. But when that theory or hypothesis was subjected to testing, the context of justification dictated that only the logic of knowledge mattered. This sharp distinction has been found wanting on several grounds and *postpositivist* philosophy is broadly concerned with various ways of accounting for human judgment in the testing of scientific hypotheses. **See also** SUBJECTIVE/SUBJECTIVITY, TACIT (PERSONAL) KNOWLEDGE, THEORY.

KEY INFORMANT   Anthropological and sociological fieldworkers often distinguish respondents from informants. The former are simply subjects, relatively unknown to the fieldworker, individuals who provide information by allowing themselves to be either observed, interviewed, or both. Informants, on the other hand, have a special relationship with the fieldworker. This relationship or role is often cultivated by the fieldworker; an informant is identified, selected, and trained to the role. Informants are knowledgeable, articulate 'insiders' possessing a unique perspective on social action in the site where the *fieldwork* is unfolding. They become the confidant and trusted advisor of the fieldworker, developing a special bond of trust. They act as a fieldwork assistant, debriefer, and guide, and often provide the fieldworker with information on what he or she cannot experience. Rapport characterizes the fieldworker's relationship with respondents, whereas friendship is more likely with informants. The growing interest in the politics of fieldwork and the concern for more careful, thoughtful exploration of self-other relationships is causing reexamination of the definition of informant in several ways: (1) Although not denying that participants in a particular social setting have their own special perspectives on the action in that setting, postmodern ethnographers are questioning whether the idea of 'informant' is not yet another way to objectify the Other or to use the Other as an extension of the imperialist gaze of the ethnographer. (2) Advocates of participatory approaches to research aim to recast all parties to a study as coparticipants rather than classify them as respondents, informants, researchers, and so on. This is more than a semantic distinction; it signals a democratic impulse underlying the inquiry and a different goal of the inquiry process. (3) Some feminist researchers, particularly those committed to action research and participatory inquiry, argue for identification with those one studies and putting the researcher 'on the same plane' as the respondent. **See also** RESPONDENT.

K

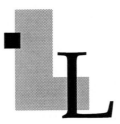

LANGUAGE GAMES   The philosophy of *logical positivism* was rejected by (among others) a group of analytic or linguistic philosophers collectively labeled "ordinary language philosophers." One
strand of this philosophy of particular importance to social inquiry
is often traced to the ideas of Ludwig Wittgenstein's (1889-1951) later
writings, particularly his *Philosophical Investigations* (1952). Here, in
an apparent rejection of his earlier views, Wittgenstein advanced the
notion that words have meanings only within diverse language
games that are forms of life (combinations of intentions, motivations,
speech, action, interests, and so on). Thus, the significance and
meaning of concepts like 'truth' and 'knowledge' are not to be found
in a logical analysis of language but rather are fixed by different
linguistic practices. The philosopher Peter Winch (*The Idea of a Social
Science and Its Relation to Philosophy*, Routledge and Kegan Paul, 1958)
linked the notion of language games to the notion of *Verstehen* to

further support a fundamental difference between the natural and social (or human) sciences: "the notion of a human society involves a scheme of concepts which is logically incompatible with the kinds of explanations offered in the natural sciences" (p. 72).

What is notable here for understanding something of the roots of qualitative inquiry in the social sciences is not Winch's work per se, for it has been subject to severe criticisms. Rather, what matters more is the idea of language games and the play of usages of words in different language games and the broad turn away from the scientific philosophy of logical positivism and its methods. Variations on the idea of examining language-in-use or how linguistic practices shape social reality are foundational to much of what we identify as the tradition of qualitative inquiry. Investigations of the politics, rhetoric and poetics of language, narrative epistemology, interpretations as constitutive of being human, and so on are definitive of the kinds of investigations we typically call 'qualitative.' When the ordinary language philosophers loosened the grip of scientific philosophy as <u>the</u> way to think about the relationship between social science and philosophy, it became possible to explore other avenues of philosophical thought as relevant to understanding social inquiry. These included Friedrich Nietzsche's (1844-1900) skepticism about the relationship of language to reality; Benjamin Lee Whorf's (1897-1941) hypothesis of linguistic relativism (every language expresses and creates a distinct and autonomous system of thought); C. S. Peirce's (1839-1914) semiotics; John Dewey's (1859-1952) pragmatism; Ferdinand Saussure's (1857-1913) linguistics; and more recently Jacques Derrida's deconstructionism, among other sources. The most radical understanding of language games is held by some postmodernists and poststructuralists who claim that all of reality is linguistic convention. John Patrick Diggins (*The Promise of Pragmatism: Modernism and the Crisis of Knowledge and Authority*, Univ. of Chicago Press, 1994, p. 435) provides a brief and not particularly charitable summary of this view as "the conviction that all human cognition is inescapably verbal or textual and consists of a web of unstable, dancing signifiers having no reference to a reality beyond the text; words full of sound and fury signifying not nothing but almost everything, as though the script were out of control; philosophers assuming they are looking for truth and waking up to realize

L

they are only writing words about words, manipulating metaphors, alternating verbal images." **See also** POSTSTRUCTURALISM, TEXT.

LAWLIKE GENERALIZATION   Lawlike does not mean 'almost a law'; rather the terms "lawlike" or "nomological" are meant to distinguish generalizations that have the force of laws from those that are merely accidental. Generalizations that have lawlike force state what <u>must</u> be the case. I might claim 'All the books on the bookshelf in my office are published in the United States.' (A generalization because it is in the form 'All Xs are As.') That may in fact be true, but its truth is accidental; the statement does not possess the quality of unrestricted necessity. **See also** GENERALIZATION.

LEBENSWELT   See LIFE-WORLD.

LIFE-HISTORY METHODOLOGY   Also called the biographical method, this is a generic term for a variety of approaches to qualitative study that focus on the generation, analysis, and presentation of the data of a life history (the unfolding of an individual's experiences over time), life story, personal experience narrative, autobiography, and biography. Data can be generated from interviews as well as from personal documents (letters, journals, diaries, and so forth). The methodology assumes that human action can best be understood from the accounts and perspectives of the people involved, and thus the focus is on an individual subjective definition and experience of life. Because, however, most qualitative inquirers assume that the subjective world of experience is at once intersubjectively constituted, life-history approaches seek to interrelate the private and the public, the personal and the social. Private, subjective perspectives are linked to meanings, definitions, concepts, and practices that are public and social. The methodology takes up a number of interrelated methodological, philosophical, and epistemological concerns surrounding what constitutes a life, a self, experience and how to best describe, interpret, and write a life-history text. For an overview of these considerations including how the approach is shaped by assumptions from phenomenological, hermeneutic, semiotic, and poststructural perspectives, see Norman K. Denzin, Chap. 8, in *The Research Act*, 3rd ed., Prentice Hall, 1989; *Interpretive Biography*, Sage, 1989; *Interpretive Interactionism*, Sage, 1989.

LIFE-WORLD The everyday world or the life-world (*Lebenswelt*) is the intersubjective world of human experience and social action; it is the world of common sense knowledge of everyday life. It is constituted by the thoughts and acts of individuals and the social expressions of those thoughts and acts (e.g., laws, institutions). The life-world is regarded as the primary object for study by the human sciences. Describing what the life-world consists of, that is what are the structures of experience and the principles and concepts that give form and meaning to the life-world, has been the project of *phenomenology*. Edmund Husserl (1859-1938) (*The Crisis of European Sciences and Transcendental Phenomenology*, trans. D. Carr, Northwestern Univ. Press, 1970) claimed that the life-world was the basis for meaning in every science; in all natural and social science (as well as logic and mathematics) the life-world is presupposed and pregiven. Husserl's transcendental phenomenological philosophy sought to explain the existence and meaning of the life-world. He distinguished between the "natural attitude," characteristic of our being in the life-world— our everyday relatively unproblematic involvement with people, things, the world—and the "phenomenological attitude," the philosophical act of pure reflection in which we suspend, distance ourselves from, or bracket all the intentions, awareness, and convictions characteristic of the natural attitude. This posture Husserl called the transcendental *epoché* ("transcendental" meaning literally to get beyond or transcend the limits of ordinary experience). Husserl argued that by making the phenomenological reduction, moving back from the natural attitude to the phenomenological attitude, we are capable of recognizing the true nature and meaning of the life-world, its ultimate transcendental ground which, in Husserl's view, was the transcendental ego (a quite complex notion in Husserl's philosophy). Building on Husserl's work, but relinquishing somewhat the attachment to phenomenological psychology and transcendental philosophy, Alfred Schutz (1899-1956) attempted to develop a descriptive phenomenology of the life-world or a phenomenological sociology. In *The Phenomenology of the Social World* (trans. G. Walsh and F. Lehnert, Northwestern Univ. Press, 1967) and in his *Collected Papers* (Martinus Nijhoff, 1967) Schutz analyzed the concepts of subjective meaning, action, experience, intentionality, behavior, and intersubjectivity and thereby sought to develop a theory that ex-

L

plained the life-world. (For a brief summary and critique of some of Schutz's major ideas as they relate to defining the aim of social inquiry, see R. J. Bernstein, *The Restructuring of Social and Political Theory*, Part III, Univ. of Pennsylvania Press, 1976.) **Philosophical hermeneutics** is also concerned with understanding the principles and organization of the life-world but from a somewhat different perspective. Rather than portray the structures or features of the life-world, philosophical hermeneutics is concerned with understanding how we are part of or engaged with that world and how conditions of our engagement (e.g., language, the nature and structures of communication) make interpreting that world an inescapable feature of our existence. **See also** HUMAN ACTION, MULTIPLE REALITIES, PHENOMENOLOGICAL SOCIOLOGY.

LITERARY TURN (IN SOCIAL SCIENCE)   This phrase refers to the growing interest in recent decades in examining the literary or rhetorical features of the texts produced by social inquirers. It does not, however, simply point to a form of literary criticism concerned only with tropes, narrative strategies, and other textual devices. Rather, it reflects the assumption that writing is central to what social inquirers do both in the field and after, and that writing about others is part of the complex process of social construction and reconstruction of reality. The literary turn introduced the idea that sociological and anthropological texts are fiction—that is, made or crafted by the inquirer—and thus shaped by rhetorical, political, institutional, and disciplinary conventions. The examination of fieldwork texts as literature is intimately linked to the issue of *representation.* It challenges naive *ethnographic realism* and assumptions about transparency of representation and the immediacy and authenticity of field experience. Within the literary turn, the examination of written texts becomes a means of addressing questions about the methodology, epistemology, politics, authority, and ethics of the activity of social inquiry. Literary processes—for example, metaphor, figuration, narrative—at work in texts are explored to understand how they help constitute the inquirer-as-author and the *human action* and people he or she seeks to represent. **See also** TEXT, VOICE.

LOGICAL EMPIRICISM   This mid-twentieth century, more moderate version of *logical positivism* informs contemporary mainstream thinking in the philosophy of social science. It is represented in the work of Ernest Nagel (1901-1985), *The Structure of Science: Problems in the Logic of Scientific Explanation* (Routledge and Kegan Paul, 1961); Hans Reichenbach (1891-1953), *Experience and Prediction* (Univ. of Chicago Press, 1938) and *The Rise of Scientific Philosophy* (Univ. of California Press, 1951); Rudolph Carnap (1891-1970), *The Logical Structure of the World* (1967; first appeared in 1928 as *Die Logische Aufbau der Welt*); Carl Hempel, *Philosophy of Natural Science* (Prentice Hall, 1966); and to some extent Karl Popper (1902-1994) in *The Logic of Scientific Discovery* (1958; originally *Logik der Forschung*, 1935). Three ideas central to this view are (1) the *covering-law model of explanation*, (2) the unity of sciences thesis, and (3) the distinction between the context of discovery and the context of justification. Logical empiricists hold that the aim of science is the development of theoretical explanations and that legitimate explanations, in turn, take the form of general (covering) laws; events to be explained are subsumed under covering laws. The controversy over what constitutes a legitimate scientific explanation and whether there can be laws in social science centers around the defense and critique of this central logical empiricist idea (see, for example, the collection of papers in Part II of *Readings in the Philosophy of Social Science*, M. M. Martin and L. C. McIntyre, eds., MIT Press, 1994). Logical empiricists also argue for the unity of the sciences, claiming that both natural and social sciences have the same aim and that there are no basic methodological differences between the two. They believe that philosophers like Wilhelm Dilthey (1833-1911), Max Weber (1864-1920), Alfred Schutz (1899-1956), Peter Winch, and others who claimed that there was a fundamental difference between explanation and understanding as goals of the natural and social sciences, respectively, were mistaken. In their view, the idea of pursuing an understanding of the 'meaning' of *human action* was a residue of metaphysical thinking. Finally, logical empiricists also draw a sharp line between the process involved in creating a theory or hypothesis (context of discovery) and the process required for testing that theory or hypothesis (context of justification). This distinction along with the covering-law model of explanation and the naturalism of logical empiricism, are the foils for hermeneutic and phenomenological approaches to social inquiry. Despite a variety of severe criticisms of it within the philosophy of science, the generalized picture of logical empiricism has become something of a vision of what the social sciences should be. For a brief critique of this view see the introduction to P. Rabinow and W. M. Sullivan, eds., *Interpretive Social Science: A Second Look,* Univ. of California Press, 1987. **See also** **EXPLANATION, NATURALISM, THEORY.**

LOGICAL POSITIVISM   From about 1922 to 1940 a group of philosophers and scientists that came to be known as the Vienna Circle developed a philosophy of science they called logical positivism. This philosophy is a particular species of analytic or linguistic philosophy preoccupied with scientific philosophy, that is, it aimed to solve a special set of problems arising out of the activity and claims of the natural sciences. Its method was that of transcendental analysis of scientific language—analyzing concepts, propositions, and scientific sentences to develop a transparent linguistic framework modeled on formal logic. It sought to discover the uniform logical structure of language and thus establish the foundation for all knowledge claims about the world. From the positivist philosophy of Auguste Comte (1798-1857) and the *empiricism* of David Hume (1711-1776) the logical positivists appropriated the idea of a strong critique of *metaphysics* and a devotion to the value of empirical observations. From the analytic philosophers Ludwig Wittgenstein (1889-1951), whose *Tractatus Logico-Philosophicus* first appeared in 1921, Bertrand Russell (1872-1970), *Introduction to Mathematical Philosophy,* 1919, and Alfred North Whitehead (1861-1947), coauthor with Russell of the three-volume *Principia Mathematica,* 1910-1913, the logical positivists developed the idea of constructing a logically correct language that would readily distinguish between meaningful and meaningless scientific propositions. (Note, however, that Wittgenstein, Russell, and Whitehead were not positivists and rejected the scientistic, empiricistic philosophy of the Vienna Circle.)

This philosophy rested on the central notion that there are only two legitimate forms of scientific inquiry that yield genuine knowledge: logical analysis and empirical research. Although there was not complete unanimity in the outlook of the group, generally they endorsed three central doctrines: (1) The verification theory of meaning: To be considered genuine, legitimate, and meaningful a knowledge claim about the world must be capable of verification through experience; (2) The doctrine of meaningful statements: Only two kinds of statements are of any value in scientific knowledge—the analytic statements of mathematics and logic, which are knowable a priori, and synthetic or contingent statements, which are knowable a posteriori based on verification through observation. Statements that are not capable of expression in either of these forms are at best irrelevant to scientific knowledge and at worst meaningless. Hence, logical positivism was extremely hostile to theological and metaphysical speculation about the world. In fact, the logical positivists disdained the appellation 'positivists' because they felt that August Comte's philosophy of science was entirely too metaphysical. (3) A foundationalist epistemology: All justified belief ultimately rests on noninferential self-evident observations (protocol statements or observation statements). This philosophy enjoyed about a 30-year life before the weight of criticisms of these doctrines caused its internal collapse. It developed into a more moderate philosophy called logical empiricism. For a brief history of this philosophy, which survives in spirit despite having been subjected to devastating criticisms by philosophers, see the introduction to A. J. Ayers, *Logical Positivism* (Free Press, 1959). **See also POSITIVISM, LOGICAL EMPIRICISM.**

LOGOCENTRISM   See DECONSTRUCTIONISM.

M

MARGINAL NATIVE See PARTICIPANT OBSERVATION.

MATERIALIST EXPLANATION See EXPLANATION.

MEMBER CHECK Also called member or respondent validation, this is a sociological term for soliciting feedback from respondents on the inquirer's findings. It is often claimed to be an important procedure for corroborating or verifying one's findings or of ensuring they meet the criterion of *confirmability.* Many researchers, however, see it as a problematic notion in several respects. First, on epistemic grounds, it is not entirely clear how the procedure actually helps establish the truth of findings. Suppose, for example, that a member check yields a difference of opinion between the inquirer and respondents, respondents disagreeing with some or all aspects of the inquirer's findings, interpretations, or both. The inquirer must then do further checking to explore the nature of the disagreement; for example, are respondents disagreeing to protect something—do they actually accept that the findings are correct but do not wish them to be made public because the findings somehow cast respondents in a bad light or are unbalanced, slanted in favor of something negative or positive, and so on; are respondents agreeing because they haven't actually taken the time to inspect the findings; are respondents disagreeing because the inquirer made an error in interpretation (if so, what kind of error, how can it be remedied); and so on? Hence, rather than being some kind of simple corroboration or act of validation by respondents, member checking seems but one more opportunity to gather data about the integrity of the inquirer's findings. Second, implementing member checking may be coupled with the assumption that researcher effects must be minimized. On this view, the researcher must guard against doing anything in the field that would influence respondents or change their behaviors or opinions. This, of course, assumes that the inquirer must stand apart from the world he or she studies. Thus, in doing member checking the inquirer must somehow guard against introducing bias. But member checking assumes a quite different character and meaning to the extent that the inquiry becomes a more participative and dialogical undertaking and less the monological activity of the lone fieldworker doing research on respondents. Third, member checking may be more of an ethical act than an epistemological one. In other words, it may simply be the civil thing to do for those who have given their time and access to their lives to give them the courtesy of knowing (or to honor their right to know) what the inquirer has to say about them. The consensus seems to be that member checking is not profitably viewed as an act of either validation or refutation but is simply another way of generating data and insight. **See also** VALIDITY.

M

MEMOING   A procedure suggested by Barney Glaser (*Theoretical Sensitivity: Advances in the Methodology of Grounded Theory,* Sociology Press, 1978) for explaining or elaborating on the coded categories that the fieldworker develops in analyzing data. Memos are conceptual in intent, vary in length, and are primarily written to oneself. The content of memos can include commentary on the meaning of a coded category, explanation of a sense of pattern developing among categories, a *description* of some specific aspect of a setting or phenomenon, and so forth. Memos capture the thoughts of the inquirer while he or she is engaged in the process of analysis. Typically, the final analysis and interpretation is based on integration and analysis of memos. For additional details on the procedure see M. Miles and A. M. Huberman, *Qualitative Data Analysis*, 2nd ed., Sage, 1994; J. Lofland and L. H. Lofland, *Analyzing Social Settings*, 3rd ed., Wadsworth, 1995. **See also ANALYZING QUALITATIVE DATA.**

METAETHNOGRAPHY   A term coined by George Noblit and R. Dwight Hare (*Metaethnography: Synthesizing Qualitative Studies*, Sage, 1988) for the process of creating new interpretations from the synthesis of multiple field studies. Although this idea is something of a qualitative analog to the notion of statistical metanalysis, the authors emphasize that metaethnographic inquiry is interpretive, not aggregative or analytical. They describe three strategies for analysis: reciprocal translation of one study into the terms of another; refutational synthesis—opposing the claims of two or more studies; and, lines-of-argument synthesis in which the interpreter engages in something like grounded theorizing, combining parts of various studies into an integrated whole. Their procedures are useful in doing both literature reviews and comparative or cross-case analysis. **See also CROSS-CASE ANALYSIS.**

METAPHYSICS   This is the study of reality, of being, of the real nature of whatever is, of first principles. Sometimes called ontology (although some philosophers define ontology as a branch of metaphysics), it is concerned with understanding the kinds of things that constitute the world. For example, Platonism is a theory of metaphysical dualism: There is the world of matter—appearances, everyday life, the senses—and the world of mind—true realities, the objects of the intellect. Cartesian metaphysics posits a somewhat different mind-body dualism: Human beings are composed of the mental and the material. Much contemporary psychology assumes a metaphysical distinction between an inner mental life and outer physical behavior, although Descartes (1596-1650) never proposed the distinction in this way. *Idealism* is a metaphysics as well. One version of idealism holds that nothing exists but minds and their content, the experience of minds. Another version acknowledges that there are material things in the world as well as minds, but seeks to reduce matter to mind by arguing that the universe is constituted by mind. Martin Heidegger's (1889-1976) metaphysics, central to the work of Hans-Georg Gadamer and *philosophical hermeneutics,* is aimed at understanding *Dasein* or human-being-in-the world. Edmund Husserl's (1859-1938) phenomenology, a metaphysics concerned with the essential structures of conscious experience, strongly influenced Alfred Schutz (1899-1956), whose work in turn provides the philosophical basis for *phenomenological sociology* and *ethnomethodology.*

The logical positivists were openly hostile to metaphysics—to any philosophical claims about reality, truth, being, and so on. They argued that metaphysical claims were incapable of being judged as true or false and thus of no consequence for increasing scientific knowledge of the world. For an example of how logical positivists employed tools for logical analysis of language to thereby reveal metaphysics to be meaningless see the chapter by Rudolph Carnap in A. J. Ayer, ed., *Logical Positivism,* Free Press, 1959.

METHOD A seemingly innocent term, "method" has several different connotations depending on the philosophical framework within which it is employed. First, in the everyday, ordinary usage of the term in qualitative studies (and social inquiry more generally) "method" denotes a procedure, tool, or technique used by the inquirer to generate data, analyze data, or both. These tools may be used during *fieldwork* and when one leaves the field and engages in *deskwork.* Typically, we think of three kinds of tools to generate qualitative data: *interviewing* (listening, talking, conversing), *participant observation* (watching), and *document analysis* (reading). Qualitative inquiry, however, is by no means limited to these tools. Many fieldworkers find it useful to generate data through structured questionnaires, surveys, standardized measurement instruments, unobtrusive observation, photography, and videotaping, to name a few. Tools for analyzing qualitative data are equally varied and include displays, taxonomies, typologies, constant comparison, enumeration, analytic induction, content analysis, and univariate and bivariate statistical analyses.

This cornucopia of methods available to qualitative inquirers does not simply point to eclecticism of method. Rather, it signals the fact that qualitative inquiry is not defined by a preoccupation with a particular method: There is no one method or set of methods that if adopted define a particular inquiry as *qualitative.* This claim is what makes many who think of themselves as rigorous social scientists desire to remove themselves as far as possible from what they see as the madding crowd of qualitative inquirers. For, given the lingering influence of *logical empiricism* in American social science, it is commonplace to assume that what defines an undertaking as truly scientific (i.e., what leads to genuine, rational, objective explanation) is, in large part, reliance on strict rules of procedure and method. Method, so conceived, is essential to the characterization of an inquiry as scientific and to the validation of its claims to know.

This leads to a second and more profound way of understanding the term "method"— as in 'scientific method.' Or, perhaps more accurately, it leads to considering an often overlooked set of assumptions that define the typical understanding of method. A modern, Cartesian, or Enlightenment conception of method assumes a subject-object dichotomy. It begins from the belief that we should separate the mind (the knower, consciousness) from the thing (that to be known, the object of consciousness). In this way of thinking, the function of method is to bracket *bias* or prejudice and keep the object of understanding at arm's length, where it can be observed safely with disinterest and lack of involvement. Thus, it is not the subjectivity of the inquirer that produces knowledge but the method. Defenders of this idea argue that is precisely <u>because</u> method functions in this way that we are able to acquire an objective, rational *explanation* of the way the world really is (i.e., the truth about the world) free of the predilections, eccentricities, prejudices and characteristics of age, social location, race, class, gender, and ethnicity that define the inquirer. In other words, genuine, legitimate knowledge is limited to methodically self-conscious knowledge. Because this notion of method is so central to the activity of knowing in social science, it is not surprising that so much criticism is directed toward method. This understanding of method is alive and well in some versions of qualitative inquiry that trace their allegiances to the

Verstehen tradition in sociology and the *phenomenological sociology* of Alfred Schutz (1988-1956).

Different understandings of method follow from critiques of this modern or Cartesian conception. Defenders of *philosophical hermeneutics* (e.g., Gadamer, Taylor) seek to undermine the central place that method occupies in defining what constitutes knowledge. They model knowledge on practical reason, dialogue, and interpretation as a fundamental condition of being human. They challenge the idea that understanding our social world is to be determined by method and that knowledge is the product of methodical consciousness. Likewise, many feminist epistemologies challenge the idea of method as requiring disengaged, detached objectivity. Postmodernists offer a more radical critique. Because, as Lyotard once noted, *postmodernism* sets out to change the meaning of the word "knowledge," and it challenges the very idea of an inquirer as knowing subject, postmodernist approaches generally reject all claims that methods (or inquirers) produce knowledge. A postmodernist inquirer may employ a 'strategy' like deconstruction but never a method. These strategies are used to further the paradox of multiple meanings and to play with an infinite variety of interpretations. **See also** DECONSTRUCTIONISM, HERMENEUTIC CIRCLE, OBJECTIVE/OBJECTIVITY.

M

METHODOLOGY   The theory of how inquiry should proceed. It involves analysis of the principles and procedures in a particular field of inquiry (that, in turn, govern the use of particular methods). The study of methodology includes topics in the philosophy of social science (e.g., explanation, theory, causality, and so on) and philosophical anthropology (the study of human nature). Ethnography, for example, is the methodology associated with the discipline of anthropology; survey research is one of the methodologies associated with the discipline of sociology. The most radical of postmodernists would probably not agree, but I believe it reasonable to say that deconstructionism is the methodology of poststructuralism. "Scientific methodology" is an ill-defined term that covers a wide range of assumptions governing what might be called a standard view of social science. Although it is arguable whether there is any longer (or ever was) such a standard view, there are attempts to portray the basic concepts of a scientific methodology in most research methods textbooks in the social sciences. The study of methodology includes examination of general theories about human behavior, society, and, more broadly, human nature itself; specific hypotheses about what phenomena are important to study; assumptions about the relationship between warrants, evidence, the nature of inferences, and what constitutes legitimate knowledge; assumptions about the integrity, completeness, and thoroughness of various data sources; assumptions about causality; and so on. The study of methodology helps us understand that there is much more than the use of method going on in various forms of human inquiry.

MICROETHNOGRAPHY   A particular type of qualitative inquiry specifically concerned with exhaustive, fine-grained examination of either a very small unit within an organization, group or culture (e.g., a particular classroom in a school); a specific activity within an organizational unit (e.g., how physicians communicate with elderly patients in an emergency room); or ordinary everyday conversation. **See also** ETHNOMETHODOLOGY.

MULTIPLE REALITIES   For the past several decades, there has been widespread interest in the idea that the meaning of human action and language can be grasped only in relation to some specific context or frame of reference. This is the central insight of the interpretive turn in both the natural and the social sciences. For example, Thomas Kuhn (1922-1996) (*The Structure of Scientific Revolutions*, 2nd ed., Univ. of Chicago Press, 1970) argued that paradigms were such a frame of reference in the natural sciences; Peter Winch (*The Idea of a Social Science*, Routledge and Kegan Paul, 1958) held that social action can be understood only in the context of particular forms of life or *language games* (concepts he borrowed from Ludwig Wittgenstein's [1889-1951] philosophy). Another notion that shares this basic premise is multiple realities. Originating in the psychology of William James (1842-1910), a theory of multiple realities was developed by Alfred Schutz (1889-1956) as part of his phenomenology of the *life-world* or social world in which we live. Schutz (see his *Collected Papers, Vol. 1*, trans. M. Natanson, Martinus Nijhoff, 1967, pp. 207ff.) used the idea of multiple realities or "finite provinces of meaning" to clarify the relationship between the reality of the world of everyday life and the world of scientific, theoretical contemplation. He explained that the paramount reality or primary world in which we live is the intersubjective world of daily life. It possesses a specific set of characteristics that mark its unique "cognitive style." For example, we do not doubt its existence; in it we experience a particular form of sociality; in it we have a specific time perspective; and so on. But we also live our lives in other worlds or finite provinces of meaning on which, in Schutz's words, we "bestow the accent of reality." These include the world of dreams, art, and religion, the play world of the child, the world of scientific contemplation, the world of the insane, and so on. Each of these provinces of meaning has its own "cognitive style," and as we transfer attention from one finite province to another we experience a "shock" of breaking through the "system of relevances" unique to one province to shift to the system of relevances unique to the other. Schutz pointed out that we do not necessarily select one of these provinces to live in, start from, or return to. Rather, our consciousness runs through many different shocks and adopts many different "attentional attitudes" in the course of a single day, and sometimes even a single hour. Furthermore, Schutz emphasized that these different provinces of meaning were not distinctly separable mental states or literally different "realities": "The finite provinces of meaning are not separated states of mental life in the sense that passing from one to another would require a transmigration of the soul. . . . They are merely names for different tensions in one and the same consciousness, and it is the same life, the mundane life, unbroken from birth to death, which is attended to in different modifications." Turning to the finite province of meaning called scientific contemplation, Schutz explained that its distinctive cognitive style centered on the attitude of the "disinterested observer" who turns the world into an object of contemplation. This attitude, in turn, is indispensable to scientific theorizing about the world. The scientific attitude means that the scientist puts her or his bodily existence, subjectivity, social relationships, and so on in brackets so as to adopt an attitude of total disinterested contemplation. The scientist suspends the "cognitive style" and the concerns that dominate her or his everyday life. Thus, the same individual acting in the finite province of meaning of the everyday world adopts a radically different set of relevant concerns, attitudes, and interests when acting in the finite province of meaning of scientific contemplation. A critique of this idea of the social inquirer as disinterested observer figures prominently in methodologies of qualitative inquiry that draw on critical social science, feminist theory, and ideas of participative inquiry. Likewise, *philosophical hermeneutics* is highly critical of a knowing subject radically divorced from the object of her or his contemplation.

M

NARRATIVE EPISTEMOLOGY. See NARRATIVE KNOWING (NARRA-
TIVE PSYCHOLOGY).

NARRATIVE EXPLANATION   There is a long-standing controversy
in the discipline of history over whether stories about past events
(historical narratives) explain the occurrence of those events. The
debate unfolds between defenders of formal scientific *explanation*
on one hand and proponents of a unique form of narrative understanding on the other, and thus the debate echoes the more general
argument over whether *Erklärung* or *Verstehen* is the proper goal of
social inquiry. The critical issue here is one of *epistemology,* namely
the nature and justification of knowledge claims. The classic statement of historical explanation framed in terms of the *deductive-
nomological model* is found in the article by the logical empiricist
Carl Hempel ("The Function of General Laws in History," *Journal of*

Philosophy, 1942, 39: 35-48) and defended by the historian Maurice Mandelbaum (*The Anatomy of Historical Knowledge*, Johns Hopkins Univ. Press, 1977). That view has been subjected to a variety of criticisms (see, for example, William Dray, *Laws and Explanations in History*, Oxford Univ. Press, 1957; Louis Mink, "The Autonomy of Historical Understanding," *History and Theory*, 1965, 5: 24-47; Hayden White, *Metahistory*, Johns Hopkins Univ. Press, 1973). Whether narrative explanations actually are legitimate explanations or only fictional narratives continues to be an important topic in philosophy of history (see, for example, Paul Roth, "Narrative Explanations: The Case of History," *History and Theory*, 1988, 27: 1-13). The import of this controversy for qualitative inquirers is significant given the strong current interest in narrative modes of inquiry. For a summary of the controversy over historical explanation see Chap. 3 in Donald E. Polkinghorne, *Narrative Knowing and the Human Sciences*, SUNY Press, 1988.

NARRATIVE INQUIRY   This term signals the activities involved in working with the various kinds of stories of life experiences found in life histories, long interviews, journals, diaries, memoirs, autobiographies, biographies, and the like. Narrative inquiry encompasses issues of *narrative ontology, narrative knowing, voice,* and *representation.* It is concerned with the means of generating data in the form of stories, means of interpreting that data, and means of representing it in narrative or storied form. Approaches to narrative analysis have been discussed in developmental psychology by Mark Tappan and Lyn M. Brown and in psychotherapy by Theodore Sarbin. Robert Coles's work in medical sociology (*The Call of Stories*, Houghton Mifflin, 1989) and his series of studies on the lives of women and children has done much to popularize the concept. Discussion of issues associated with narrative inquiry has become something of a new cottage industry in the field of education (see, for example, Hunter McEwan and Kieran Egan, eds., *Narrative in Teaching, Learning, and Research*, Teachers College Press, 1995; Carol Witherell and Nel Noddings, eds., *Stories Lives Tell: Dialogue and Narrative in Education*, Teachers College Press, 1991).

NARRATIVE KNOWING (NARRATIVE PSYCHOLOGY)   Narrative has been proposed as a particular cognitive function, way of thinking, or rationality. For example, Jerome Bruner (*Actual Minds, Possible Worlds*, Harvard Univ. Press, 1986, pp. 11f.) has argued that there are two distinctive ways in which we order experience. The two are complementary but not reducible to one another: the paradigmatic, logico-scientific mode and the narrative mode. The former leads to the well-formed argument that seeks to convince us of its truth through "tight analysis, logical proof, sound argument, and empirical discovery guided by reasoned hypothesis"; the latter leads to good stories that seek to convince us of their lifelikeness. Each mode of thought has different criteria for evaluating its outcome. Bruner has written about the psychology of narrative thought, particularly how it is that we construct the world through narrative. Charles Taylor (*Sources of the Self: The Making of the Modern Identity*, Harvard Univ. Press, 1989) has also argued for narrative thought as an essential aspect of practical reasoning. From the qualitative inquirer's point of view, it is the suppression of the narrative way of knowing that is of greatest concern. **See also NARRATIVE ONTOLOGY.**

NARRATIVE ONTOLOGY   Narrative ontology is concerned with the storied nature of being or a narrative theory of human existence. The expression "we lead storied lives" expresses this concern. There are many strands of thought entailed here but generally narrative ontology draws on both *phenomenology* and *ontological hermeneutics* to argue against a *metaphysics* of inner mind over against outer behavior. Narrative ontology opposes the empiricist view of experience as consisting of an internal mental reaction to an exterior physical world. It stresses instead ways in which experience is always open to the world and the complex interaction between consciousness (or being) and world (hence the use of terms like the 'fusion' of experience and world or the 'horizon' of experience). Narrative ontology is a complex idea that requires careful study to be fully appreciated, but consider the contrast between the following two viewpoints: In viewpoint A—a Cartesian conception—individual mind, consciousness, or individual being (human existence) faces a pregiven world on which it 'operates,' so to speak. Individual consciousness engages in a project of theoretical contemplation of this pregiven world. In viewpoint B, individual consciousness or individual historical being is already 'there' before individual awareness of same. In other

N

words, consciousness or being is part of the pregiven *life-world*—consciousness or being is <u>already</u> historical, temporal, and social.

Narrative ontology seeks to explain how notions of existence, self, emotions, remembering, identity, passions, thinking, time, and the like are constituted narratively or discursively. Important sources of ideas here are Edmund Husserl's (1859-1938) phenomenology of the life-world (*The Crisis of European Sciences and Transcendental Phenomenology,* trans. D. Carr, Northwestern Univ. Press, 1970), Martin Heidegger's (1889-1976) analysis of *Dasein* (human existence) in his *Being and Time* (trans. J. Macquarrie and E. Robinson, Harper & Row, 1962; originally published in 1927), and Paul Ricoeur's two-volume *Time and Narrative* (trans. K. McLaughlin and D. Pellauer, Univ. of Chicago Press, 1984-1986). The philosopher David Carr (*Time, Narrative, and History,* Indiana Univ. Press, 1986) draws on Husserl and Heidegger to explain narrative as a temporal structure inherent in our way of living and acting. Although they do not use the term "narrative" per se, Rom Harré and Grant Gilbert (*The Discursive Mind,* Sage, 1994, pp. 18ff.) single out discourse as the characteristic feature of the second revolution in cognitive psychology. Psychological phenomena are interpreted as features of public or private discourse rather than expressions of some underlying mental state. Hence, psychological phenomena (including thinking) are examined in the context of their occurrence as situated constructions created by means of interpersonal discursive processes. For a summary of important ideas in narrative ontology, see Chap. 4 in Donald E. Polkinghorne, *Narrative Knowing and the Human Sciences,* SUNY Press, 1988.

NATIVE'S POINT OF VIEW   This is one of the methodological innovations marking the emergence in the 1920s of participant observation as the scientific approach of ethnography. Earlier interpreters'—missionaries, government administrators, traders, travelers, and the like—accounts of the native life of indigenous peoples generally failed to offer the perspective as well as the practices of the members of the group themselves. By placing increased emphasis on powers of observation of events in daily life and on the collection of first-person, 'native,' or insider accounts, the methodology of *participant observation* sought to establish a firmer scientific basis for anthropological understanding. **See also** EMIC, ETHNOGRAPHIC NATURAL-ISM.

NATURALISM One of four basic approaches to the study of social phenomena (the others are antinaturalism, critical social science, and pluralism). The naturalist holds that the social or human sciences should approach the study of social phenomena with the same aim and methods as the natural sciences approach they study of natural (physical) phenomena (hence, the phrase "naturalistic interpretation of the social sciences"). In other words, the social sciences should have as their goals both prediction and causal, nomological *explanations* of human behavior. Naturalists like Karl Popper (1902-1994) and Ernest Nagel (1901-1985) admit that the search for lawlike explanations (or explanatory theory) in the social sciences may be more difficult due to the nature of the subject matter. Yet, they insist that there are no fundamental differences in kind in the explanatory goals of the natural and social sciences. For a summary of this doctrine see R. J. Bernstein, *The Restructuring of Social and Political Theory,* Univ. of Pennsylvania Press, 1976; D. Little, *Varieties of Social Explanation,* Westview Press, 1991. **See also** ANTINATURALISM, CRITICAL SOCIAL SCIENCE, PLURALISM, THEORY.

NATURALISTIC INQUIRY This is the name for a particular methodology for qualitative inquiry. In 1969, two psychologists, Edwin Willems and Harold Rausch, edited a collection of papers titled *Naturalistic Viewpoints in Psychology,* in which they defined naturalistic inquiry as "the investigation of phenomena within and in relation to their naturally occurring contexts." In 1971, Norman Denzin published the article "The Logic of Naturalistic Inquiry," in which he explained that the naturalist inquirer resists using methods that oversimplify the complexity of everyday life. In 1978, Egon Guba published the monograph *Toward a Methodology of Naturalistic Inquiry in Educational Evaluation,* in which he identified the characteristics of naturalistic inquiry and compared it with what he called more conventional (experimental and quasi-experimental) inquiry. And in 1985, Guba and Yvonna Lincoln published *Naturalistic Inquiry,* in which they contrasted "postpositivist" and "naturalist" "paradigms" on philosophical and methodological dimensions. In a subsequent formulation of their approach to qualitative studies that appeared in *Fourth Generation Evaluation* (Sage, 1989), Guba and Lincoln appear to favor the term "constructivist" to "naturalistic." What these various methodologies sharing the same name have in common is a commitment to studying human action in some setting that is not contrived, manipulated, or artificially fashioned by the inquirer; hence, the setting is said to be 'natural' or 'naturally occurring.'

Confusion with the term stems from the multiple ways in which it is used. To a philosopher of social science, **naturalism** or "naturalistic" is the name for efforts to define the aim of the social sciences as the same aim as the natural sciences. One who rejects those efforts (i.e., rejects the naturalistic interpretation of the social sciences) is an "antinaturalist." Thus, to the philosopher, those qualitative inquirers who call themselves naturalistic inquirers (because they mean "naturalistic" in the sense first defined above) are actually antinaturalists. To put it more concretely, the philosopher might say that a better title for Guba and Lincoln's book is "Antinaturalistic Inquiry." **See also** ETHNOGRAPHIC NATURALISM.

NATURALISTIC INTERPRETATION OF THE SOCIAL SCIENCES
See NATURALISM.

NATURAL SETTING   See ETHNOGRAPHIC NATURALISM, NATURALISTIC INQUIRY.

NATURWISSENSCHAFT   A German term usually translated as "natural science." **See** SCIENCE, *VERSTEHEN.*

NEGATIVE CASE   See ANALYTIC INDUCTION.

NOMOLOGICAL   See LAWLIKE GENERALIZATION.

NOMOTHETIC KNOWLEDGE   See *VERSTEHEN.*

NONFOUNDATIONAL EPISTEMOLOGY   A nonfoundationalist epistemology is one that endorses the view that it is possible and legitimate to say one 'knows' something without being absolutely certain or without recourse to ultimate proof or foundations for that knowing. Nonfoundationalists argue that all knowledge claims are fallible and subject to revision not because we have yet to find foundations but simply because that is what knowledge is. In contrast, foundationalist epistemologies assume the possibility (and necessity) of the ultimate grounding of knowledge claims and consequently search for it. *Rationalism* and *empiricism* are epistemologies concerned with the quest for certainty or foundations. *Logical positivism* was a foundationalist epistemology; it sought a sure, unshakable ground for all knowledge claims in data derived from the senses (and later in indisputable observation sentences). The quest for foundationalism is the quest for *objectivism.* **See also** **EPISTEMOLOGY.**

N

OBJECTIVE/OBJECTIVITY There are several interrelated senses of this term. (1) In traditional social scientific parlance, objectivity is often taken to be synonymous with 'methodical,' 'scientific,' 'rational,' and regarded as a quality that comes from being procedural, rule following, algorithmic. Objectivity in this sense signals the eradication of human *judgment* that is regarded as subjective. This sense of objectivity is criticized not only by defenders of *Verstehen* and *hermeneutic* approaches to the social sciences but by postempiricist philosophers of science as well (see, for example, M. Hesse, *Revolutions and Reconstructions in the Philosophy of Science*, Indiana Univ. Press, 1980; H. I. Brown, *Perception, Theory, and Commitment*, Univ. of Chicago Press, 1977). (2) Objectivity has also been defined in terms of conditions of accurate representation of reality. In this way of thinking, an account is objective to the extent that it mirrors, reflects, or represents social reality. Richard Rorty (*Objectivity, Rela-*

tivism, and Truth—Philosophical Papers, Vol. 1, Cambridge Univ. Press, 1991) is highly critical of this understanding of objectivity as are many postmodernists who hold that *representation* denies difference. The goal of much poststructural work is to reveal the deficiency and even the futility of all representational claims. (3) Objectivity is also associated with a metaphysical and epistemological separation of subject and object, as Richard J. Bernstein (*Beyond Objectivism and Relativism,* Univ. of Pennsylvania Press, 1983, p. 9) explains: "What is 'out there' (object) is presumed to be independent of us (subjects), and knowledge is achieved when a subject correctly mirrors or represents objective reality." (4) In a less strict sense of the word, objectivity means the quality of being unbiased or unprejudiced; warranted, supported (warrantable, supportable); or all of these. In this sense, one can endorse the quality of being objective without being an objectivist. (5) An 'objective' fact or statement also commonly means a statement that all reasonable people would assent to or agree with.

Sustained, multifaceted criticism of the notion of scientific objectivity is central to most all *feminist epistemologies* that argue (1) apparently objective and neutral science has a sexist bias; (2) concern with objectivity has imposed a hierarchical and controlling relationship on the researcher-researched pair; and (3) holding to objectivity as a regulative ideal has meant excluding personal, subjective knowledge from consideration as legitimate knowledge (see T. E. Jayaratne and A. J. Stewart, "Quantitative and Qualitative Methods in the Social Sciences," in Mary Margaret Fonow and Judith A. Cook, eds., *Beyond Methodology: Feminist Scholarship as Lived Research,* Indiana Univ. Press, 1991). Yet, rescuing the notion of objectivity from its more deleterious practices and connotations is also a feminist concern; see, for example, Louise M. Antony and Charlotte Witt, eds., *A Mind of One's Own: Feminist Essays on Reason and Objectivity,* Westview, 1993. **See also** OBJECTIVISM, SUBJECTIVE/ SUBJECTIVITY.

OBJECTIVISM   There are two somewhat different senses of this term. (1) In *Beyond Objectivism and Relativism* (Univ. of Pennsylvania Press, 1983, p. 8), Richard J. Bernstein defined objectivism as analogous to foundationalism: "the base conviction that there is or must be some permanent, ahistorical matrix or framework to which we can ultimately appeal in determining the nature of rationality, knowledge, truth, reality, goodness, or rightness." He argues that for many scholars, the opposites of objectivism are *relativism* or radical *skepticism*. (2) In *The Logic of Practice* (Stanford Univ. Press, 1990), French sociologist Pierre Bourdieu identified objectivism as the nature of the relation between investigator (subject) and the object of investigation. Objectivism constitutes the "theoretical relation" to the world. In that relation, the social world is "a spectacle offered to an observer who takes up a 'point of view' on the action and who . . . proceeds as if it were intended solely for knowledge" (p. 52). For Bourdieu, the important contrast is between the "theoretical relation" to the world with its attendant attitude of objectification and a "practical relation" to the world. A similar view is discussed by Charles Taylor (*Sources of the Self*, Harvard Univ. Press, 1989, pp. 159 ff.), who criticizes an epistemology that privileges disengagement and control and assumes that one must not live in or through one's experience but treat it as an object. **See also** NONFOUNDATIONAL EPISTEMOLOGY, OBJECTIVE/OBJECTIVITY, SUBJECTIVISM.

OBSERVATION   Direct firsthand eye-witness accounts of everyday social action have always been regarded as essential to answering the classic fieldwork question "what's going on here?" Extended periods of observation in the field define both anthropological work dating from the 1920s and fieldwork sociology originating in the *Chicago School* tradition of the 1930s. Observation as a fieldwork method is characterized by the following traits: (1) events, actions, meanings, norms, and so on are viewed from the perspective of people being studied; (2) a premium is placed on attention to detail; (3) events and actions can be understood only when they are set within a particular social and historical context; (4) social action is regarded as processual and dynamic, not as a set of discrete events; (5) efforts are made to avoid premature imposition of theoretical notions on participants' perspectives (see A. Bryman, *Quantity and Quality in Social Research*, Unwin Hyman, 1988). Furthermore, it is generally recognized that some general theoretical framework shapes the making and interpretation of observations, for example, symbolic interactionism, semiotic conception of culture, structural-functionalism, ethnomethodology, poststructuralism. (For an overview of different theoretical perspectives on culture see J. C. Alexander and S. Seidman, eds., *Culture and Society: Contemporary Debates*, Cambridge Univ. Press, 1990; for a symbolic interactionist focus, see N. K. Denzin, *The Research Act*, 3rd ed., Prentice Hall, 1989.) Contemporary discussion of observational methods focuses on two different conceptions of observer role and identity. The traditional concept is of participant as observer who is peripherally involved or only marginally participates in the scene he or she studies. Collaborative and participatory approaches to social inquiry introduce the idea of active participation of the inquirer in the setting and sharing the role of researcher with participants. Neither identity is necessarily a 'natural' in any social setting; inquirers adopting one of these roles must actually work to establish it within a particular site. Each role also requires careful exploration of unique ethical, political, and logistical requirements. **See also PARTICIPANT OBSERVATION.**

ONTOLOGICAL HERMENEUTICS   See PHILOSOPHICAL HERMENEUTICS.

ONTOLOGY   See METAPHYSICS.

O

PARADIGM In Thomas Kuhn's (1922-1996) monograph *The Structure of Scientific Revolutions,* the term "paradigm" played a significant role in his argument about the rationality of scientific inquiry. In the years following the 1962 publication (and subsequent 1970 revision) of that monograph, it was particularly fashionable to talk about the qualitative versus quantitative 'paradigm debate' in the social sciences (although Kuhn's book did not discuss the social sciences). The term offered a convenient conceptual shorthand for pointing to apparently significant differences in methodologies. It was not always entirely clear, however, what the term actually meant in this context. Difficulty with the use of the term stems from Kuhn's own lack of conceptual clarity. Among the many uses of the term, he singled out two quite distinct definitions in responses to his critics. On one hand, a paradigm refers to a type of cognitive framework—an "exemplar" or set of shared solutions to substantive problems used by a very well-defined specific community of scientists (radio astronomers, protein chemists, solid-state physicists, and so on) both to generate and to solve puzzles in their field. Kuhn argued that the essential activity of puzzle solving could be carried out only if the community of scientists shared these concrete exemplars, for scientists solved problems by modeling them on previous puzzle solutions. Using this definition, it is doubtful that social scientists have similar kinds of paradigms that guide their work. On the other hand, Kuhn also used the term to mean a "disciplinary matrix"—commitments, beliefs, values, methods, outlooks, and so forth shared across a discipline. This sense of paradigm as a worldview or general perspective is generally what social scientists appear to have in mind when they use the term. Two critical issues are (1) what comprises different methodological paradigms or disciplinary matrices in social inquiry, for example, what are the beliefs, assumptions and values about the aim of social inquiry, self, society, human agency, method, and so forth shared by inquirers committed to postmodern versus interpretive ethnography, for example, or those committed to feminist theory or philosophical hermeneutics? and (2) how are these paradigms socially accomplished or constituted? **See also DISCURSIVE PRACTICE, METHODOLOGY.**

PARADIGMATIC KNOWLEDGE CLAIM   A typical instance, specimen, archetype, or exemplary form of a knowledge claim. What is the exemplary form of a knowledge claim in social inquiry? What kind of knowledge does social inquiry aim to produce? These questions are explored by Lorraine Code (*What Can She Know? Feminist Theory and the Construction of Knowledge,* Cornell Univ. Press, 1991, pp. 36ff.). In a *logical empiricist* framework a simple observational statement about an object—for example, 'the door is open,' 'that square object is red'—is regarded as paradigmatic and fundamental for what it means to know. More complex claims are built out of these simple observational statements. Code argues, however, that knowing other people is at least as worthy a contender for paradigmatic status as is knowledge of objects. She maintains that the former kind of knowledge is qualitatively different from simple observational claims in the following ways: (1) it assumes a different subject-object relation; (2) these claims to know are open to negotiation between

knower and 'known'; (3) the process of knowing other people requires constant learning—how to be with them, respond to them, act
toward them; (4) this kind of knowledge is never complete or fin-
ished—even if one knew all the facts about someone (or about one's
self), that would not guarantee that one would know that person as
she is.

The issue of what constitutes a specimen (paradigmatic) knowledge claim is important for conceiving of the various aims of qualitative inquiry. Forms of qualitative inquiry wedded to empiricist
assumptions generally regard simple observational claims as most
important. Code, on the other hand, argues for forms of feminist
inquiry that take seriously the notion of knowing other people as
defining what it means to seek knowledge. Approaches to qualitative inquiry that draw on *philosophical hermeneutics* echo a similar
view in arguing for practical-moral knowledge or knowledge of
praxis. Some social constructionists also hold this view. For example,
John Shotter (*Conversational Realities,* Sage, 1993, pp. 6, 19) argues
that social inquiry must shift its focus from efforts to understand
objects to understanding human beings—from an interest in epistemology to an interest in practical hermeneutics. Practical hermeneutics, in turn, examines what Shotter variously refers to as knowledge-
in-practice, knowledge-held-in-common with others, or the kind of
knowledge one has "from within" a situation, group, social institution, or society. **See also** EPISTEMOLOGY.

PARTICIPANT OBSERVATION   Although often discussed as a
method, this activity is best understood as a methodology or discursive practice that took shape in particular social and historical circumstances in anthropology in the early twentieth century (see, for
example, G. Stocking, ed., *Observers Observed: Essays on Ethnographic
Fieldwork,* Univ. of Wisconsin Press, 1983). As a methodology for
ethnographic *fieldwork,* participant observation is a procedure for
generating understanding of the ways of life of others. It requires
that the researcher engage in some relatively prolonged period of
participation in a community, group, and so on; take some part in
the daily activities of the people among whom he or she is studying;
and reconstruct their activities through the processes of *inscription,
transcription,* and *description* in *fieldnotes* made on the spot or soon

thereafter. Broadly conceived, participant observation thus includes activities of direct observation, interviewing, document analysis, reflection, analysis, and interpretation. It encompasses both logistical, ethical, and political concerns involved in entering the world of those one studies, gaining their trust, developing empathy, and understanding their ways of talking about and acting in their world. Participant observation is a means whereby the researcher becomes socialized into the group under study.

Because of this emphasis in participant observation on requiring at least partial socialization into the world one studies, it has been commonplace to insist that the participant observer adopt the stance of a marginal native or professional stranger. In this role, the field-worker always maintains some respectful distance from those studied—cultivating empathy but never sympathy, rapport but never friendship, familiarity but never full identification (i.e., 'going native'). This critical distance is required for creating an objective account of what is being studied. Hence, the participant observer is advised to always maintain something like dual citizenship—with primary allegiance to an academic culture or disciplinary home although taking up temporary residence in the culture or group being studied.

Given this brief description, it should not be difficult to see the profit in analyzing participant observation as a methodology. A host of assumptions are built in here about the nature of interaction, engagement, and human relationships; what counts as legitimate, credible, and authentic knowledge in fieldwork; what the field-worker is actually doing when he or she claims to be 'recording' observations of interactions and utterances and 'documenting' the lived realities of others; what constitutes the authority of the participant observer; and so on. It is precisely these assumptions underlying the traditional methodology of participant observation that are the object of analysis and criticism by postmodern ethnographers, feminists, and participatory action researchers. For example, postmodern ethnographers question the authority of the eyewitness participant observer to represent the lives of others; many feminists argue <u>for</u> closeness, friendship, and mutual identification with women being studied; participatory researchers argue for research <u>with</u>, not <u>on</u>, the people being studied. For an examination of the assumptions built into the emergence of participant-observation as a professional scientific norm for anthropology, see J. Clifford, "On Ethnographic Authority," *Representations*, 1983, 1(2): 118-146. **See also** ETHNOGRAPHIC NATURALISM, ETHNOGRAPHY, FIELDWORK, OBSERVATION.

PARTICIPATORY ACTION RESEARCH (PAR) A broad designation for several kinds of *action research* that place a premium on the politics and power of knowledge production and use. Participatory action researchers typically work with groups and communities experiencing or subject to control, oppression, or colonization by a more dominant group or culture. Three characteristics appear to distinguish the forms of this practice from other forms of social inquiry: (1) its participatory character—cooperation and collaboration between the researcher(s) and other participants in problem definition, choice of methods, data analysis, and use of findings. (Note: There are various kinds or ways of participating or collaborating including participants-as-researchers, participants networked to share knowledge, participants as problem formulators, researcher-as-colleague, researcher-as-participant, and so on); (2) its democratic impulse—PAR embodies democratic ideals or principles but it is not necessarily a recipe for bringing about democratic change; (3) its objective of producing both useful knowledge and action as well as consciousness raising—empowering people through the process of constructing and using their own knowledge (see, for example, P. Reason, *Participation in Human Inquiry*, Sage, 1994, pp. 47-49). PAR is also marked by tension surrounding the simultaneous realization of the aims of participant involvement, social improvement, and knowledge production. Some advocates of PAR disavow all efforts to produce general or theoretical knowledge and focus instead on the improvement of particular practices.

Summaries of current varieties of PAR can be found in W. F. Whyte, ed., *Participatory Action Research*, Sage, 1991, and the special edition of *Human Relations*, 1993, vol. 42(2), edited by M. Elden and R. Chisholm. There are several strands of action research in particular fields of application reflecting different epistemological and methodological emphases. For example, in the Scandinavian action research tradition focused on worklife, the strategies of democratic dialogues and cogenerative learning reflect different assumptions about the aim of PAR. For different views of action research see, in education, J. Elliott, *Action Research for Educational Change* (Open Univ. Press, 1991), and P. Freire, *Pedagogy of the Oppressed* (Herder & Herder, 1970); in socioeconomic development, O. Fals-Borda and M. A. Rahman, eds., *Action and Knowledge: Breaking the Monopoly with Participatory Action Research* (Intermediate Technology/Apex, 1991); in worklife, S. Toulmin and B. Gustavsen, eds., *Beyond Theory: Changing Organizations Through Participation* (John Benjamins, 1995); F. M. van Eijnatten, *The Paradigm that Changed the Work Place* (Van Gorcum, 1993).

PEER DEBRIEFING   This is a procedure whereby the fieldworker confides in trusted and knowledgeable colleagues and uses them as a sounding board for one or more purposes. The fieldworker may wish to recount ethical or political dilemmas encountered in the field and solicit colleagues' reactions or simply have colleagues serve as good listeners. Peer debriefing can also involve sharing ideas about procedures and logistics in the field to get advice and check dependability of ways of proceeding, and it can involve sharing evolving attempts at describing and analyzing qualitative data to achieve some kind of consensual validation.

PHENOMENOLOGICAL SOCIOLOGY   Known through the work of Peter Berger and Thomas Luckmann (e.g., *The Social Construction of Reality*, Anchor, 1967; P. Berger and H. Kellner, *Sociology Reinterpreted*, Doubleday, 1981), this social theory aims to describe the structures of experience or the *life-world*. Its principal architect was Alfred Schutz (1899-1956), who built on the *phenomenology* of Edmund Husserl (1859-1938) to develop a phenomenological foundation for Weber's idea of meaningful *social action*. Schutz aimed to explain how it is that the life-world is actually produced and experienced by individuals. He sought to explain the essence of what he called the 'natural attitude'—the fact that we do not doubt the existence of the everyday world and its *intersubjective*, social character. Phenomenological sociology is thus concerned with "how we come to interpret others and their actions; with the complex ways in which we understand those with whom we interact; and with the ways in which we interpret our own actions and those of others within a social context" (R. J. Bernstein, *The Restructuring of Social and Political Theory*, Univ. of Pennsylvania Press, 1976, p. 141). Schutz argued that to effectively study the everyday world, the social inquirer must bracket or suspend one's taken-for-granted attitude toward its existence; the inquirer must assume the attitude of a disinterested observer. For brief summaries of Schutz's philosophy see Bernstein (noted previously) and A. Giddens, *New Rules of Sociological Method*, 2nd ed., Stanford Univ. Press, 1993. Schutz's major works include *The Phenomenology of a Social World*, Northwestern Univ. Press, 1967; *Collected Papers*, 3 vols., M. Natanson, ed., Martinus Nijhoff, 1973; *The Structures of the Life-World* (with T. Luckmann) Northwestern Univ. Press, 1973. **See also MULTIPLE REALITIES, PHENOMENOLOGY,** *VERSTEHEN.*

PHENOMENOLOGY   This complex, multifaceted philosophy defies simple characterization because it is not a single unified philosophical standpoint. It includes the transcendental phenomenology of Edmund Husserl (1859-1938), the existential forms of Maurice Merleau-Ponty (1908-1961) and Jean-Paul Sartre (1905-1980), and the hermeneutic phenomenology of Martin Heidegger (1889-1976). Generally speaking, phenomenologists reject scientific *realism* and the accompanying view that the empirical sciences have a privileged position in identifying and explaining features of a mind-independent world. Phenomenologists are opposed to the empiricist idea that genuine legitimate knowledge can be had only by rejecting the way we perceive the world of everyday life as 'mere appearance.' Hence, phenomenologists insist on careful description of ordinary conscious experience of everyday life (the *life-world*), a description of 'things' (the essential structures of consciousness) as one experiences them. These 'things' we experience include perception (hearing, seeing, and so on), believing, remembering, deciding, feeling, judging, evaluating, all experiences of bodily action, and so forth. Phenomenological descriptions of such things are possible only by turning from things to their meaning, from what is to the nature of what is. This turning away can be accomplished only by a certain phenomenological reduction or *epochē* that entails 'bracketing' or suspending what Husserl calls the "natural attitude." The natural attitude is the everyday assumption of the independent existence of what is perceived and thought about. (See, for example, Michael

Hammond, Jane Howarth, and Russell Keat, *Understanding Phenomenology*, Blackwell, 1991). The two major variants of phenomenology that are manifest in contemporary qualitative methodologies are the hermeneutic and the existential. The former, perhaps best known through the work of Hans-Georg Gadamer and Paul Ricoeur, tends to focus on the collective or intersubjective features of sociopolitical life as evident in the primary concern with issues of language and the nature and structure of communication. The latter variant is perhaps best known to social scientists through the work of the phenomenological sociologist Alfred Schutz (1899-1956), a colleague of Husserl, who considerably influenced the social constructionist views of Peter Berger and Thomas Luckmann (*The Social Construction of Reality*, Anchor, 1967) and the development of *ethnomethodology* by Harold Garfinkel and Aaron Cicourel. This kind of phenomenology is more oriented toward describing the experience of everyday life as it is internalized in the subjective consciousness of individuals. **See also** LIFE-WORLD, PHENOMENOLOGICAL SOCIOLOGY.

PHILOSOPHICAL HERMENEUTICS   Also called hermeneutic philosophy and ontological hermeneutics, this is the approach developed by Hans-Georg Gadamer (*Truth and Method*, 2nd rev. ed., Crossroads, 1990; originally published in German in 1960, first English translation 1975). Philosophical hermeneutics is neither a method nor a methodology for obtaining knowledge and is not based on a traditional subject-object dualism. It assumes that understanding an object (a *text*, a work of art, *human action*, another speaker, and so on) and interpreting it are essentially the same undertaking. Following the work of Martin Heidegger (1889-1976), Gadamer argues that hermeneutics is ontological, universal, and 'conversational': ontological because 'understanding' is our very mode of being in the world; universal because understanding underlies all human activity; 'conversational' because the interpretation of an object is always a dialogical encounter—as interpreters we participate in, open ourselves to, share in, and listen to the claims that the object is making on us. Understanding is always open and anticipatory; one never achieves a final, complete interpretation. This is so because we are always interpreting in light of 'prejudice' (or prejudgment, preconception) that comes from the tradition of which we are part. This tradition does not stand apart from our thought but constitutes the 'horizon' in which we do our thinking. Furthermore, language is the medium of all understanding in philosophical hermeneutics. Language is not understood as an instrument or tool but an activity that, like play, reflects an intentionality and allows for both the constitution of meaning and the instability of meaning (see the discussion of language as play in S. Gallagher, *Hermeneutics and Education*, SUNY Press, 1992). Philosophical hermeneutics has also been characterized as a hermeneutics of trust because it reflects the belief that meaning or truth will be found through interpretation modeled on dialogue and conversation. It is thus often contrasted with a *hermeneutics of suspicion.* Central ideas in Gadamer's hermeneutics are explained in Richard J. Bernstein, *Beyond Objectivism and Relativism*, Univ. of Pennsylvania Press, 1983. Other important contributions to philosophical hermeneutics are made by Charles Taylor (*Philosophical Papers, Vols. 1 and 2*, Cambridge Univ. Press, 1985) and Paul Ricoeur (*Hermeneutics and the Human Sciences*, ed. and trans. J. B. Thompson, Cambridge Univ. Press, 1981), although Ricoeur's work is sometimes discussed under the label 'phenomenological hermeneutics' (see Josef Bleicher, *Contemporary Hermeneutics: Hermeneutics as Method, Philosophy and Critique*, Routledge and Kegan Paul, 1980). **See also** HERMENEUTIC CIRCLE.

PLURALISM   One of four basic approaches to the study of social phenomena (the others are *antinaturalism, naturalism, critical social science*). Pluralists maintain that antinaturalist and naturalist approaches to the study of social life are complementary or compatible. They see no real difficulty with a social science that seeks both to explain human action and to interpret its meaning. A common view is that explanatory (naturalist) and interpretive (antinaturalist) approaches are compatible because each illuminates a different aspect of *human action* necessary for a complete understanding. For statements of methodological pluralism, see D. Braybrooke, *Philosophy of Social Science*, Prentice Hall, 1987; D. Little, *Varieties of Social Explanation*, Westview, 1991; P. Roth, *Meaning and Method in Social Science: A Case for Pluralism*, Cornell Univ. Press, 1987. **See also** EXPLANATION, *VERSTEHEN.*

POLITICS OF RESEARCH   Topics in the politics of qualitative inquiry include examination of the political forces that operate <u>on</u> the enterprise of research from the outside, so to speak, to influence the choice of questions, topics, methods, and so on; the micropolitics of relating to people in field settings; the sociopolitical stance of individual inquirers; and the politics that act <u>through</u> the enterprise of inquiry. Arguably, it is the latter two topics that are receiving the greatest attention at the present time. Hermeneutic, feminist, neo-Marxist, participatory, and some poststructuralist perspectives all challenge two long-standing political images of the social inquirer: (1) the liberal scholar who is committed to the ideal of knowledge for knowledge's sake, and (2) the *disinterested social scientist* who views her or his task as that of developing and testing empirical explanations of the social world, not changing that world. Furthermore, a number of scholars of different philosophical persuasions have drawn attention to the manner in which politics act through the social practice of research itself. They aim to theorize the activity of social inquiry not in epistemological terms but as social agency. Hence, they explore social inquiry as an economic, political, and social institution that accrues and exercises power to define the sociopolitical world. For example, Dorothy Smith (*Texts, Facts, and Femininity: Exploring the Relations of Ruling*, Routledge and Kegan Paul, 1990, p. 2) identifies sociology as one of the "ruling apparatuses of society—those institutions of administration, management, and professional authority and of intellectual and cultural discourses which organize, regulate, lead, and direct capitalist societies."

Social scientists participate in the construction of ruling relations not by exercising social authority to command obedience or control decisions about policy but by virtue of the epistemological or cognitive authority of their discipline or profession. Paul Starr (*The Social Transformation of American Medicine*, Basic Books, 1982) describes the authority of professions as cultural authority—the probability that their particular definitions of reality and judgments of meaning and value will prevail as true and valid. Charles Lindbloom (*Inquiry and Change*, Yale Univ. Press, 1990) argues that contemporary industrialized societies tend to be scientifically guided societies that look to the expertise of social scientists for social problem solving, social betterment, and guided social change. This role for social science in

P

society leads to what Dorothy Smith (*The Conceptual Practices of Power*, Northeastern Univ. Press, 1990) calls a conceptual practice of power; a power to define the sociopolitical world through objectified knowledge. This power is exercised not simply in the 'scientific' pronouncements (theories, claims) of social science professionals but through the metaphysical commitments that are reflected in social scientific activity itself. In other words, social scientists do not simply teach us their scientific views, they also convey their beliefs about the sociopolitical world. A classic illustration about such teaching is provided in Kathryn Pyne Addelson's ("The Man of Professional Wisdom," in S. Harding and M. B. Hintikka, eds., *Discovering Reality*, D. Reidel, 1983, p. 176) explanation of how the functionalist Robert Merton and the symbolic interactionist Howard Becker define the phenomenon of deviance very differently: "Merton looked for the cause of deviant behavior . . . and found the cause in social structures exerting a definite pressure on some people. Becker asks about deviant behavior as behavior defined under ban, and so he asks about who does the banning, how the ban is maintained, and what effect the ban has on the activity itself. On the basis of interactionist metaphysics, he does not assume that deviance is something there for the natural scientific eye to discern. Whether something is deviant or normal in a society is a question of power and perspective within the society."

Scholars concerned with the ways in which politics act through the institution of social science argue that social inquiry has been depoliticized: To depoliticize a practice of cognitive authority is to close the question of authority in favor of the experts, whereas to politicize the expertise of social science professionals is to open the question of cognitive authority to the critical scrutiny of society at large (see Steve Fuller, *Social Epistemology*, Indiana Univ. Press, 1988). Sandra Harding ("After the Neutrality Ideal: Science, Politics, and 'Strong Objectivity,' " *Social Research*, 1992, 59(3): 567-587) explains that the kind of politics that act less visibly and less consciously through the dominant institutional structures, priorities, practices, and languages of science paradoxically function as a kind of depoliticalization. A depoliticized practice, in Harding's view, "certifies as value-neutral, normal, natural, and not political at all the existing scientific policies and practices through which powerful groups can gain the information and explanations that they need to advance their priorities."

POSITIVISM   A term coined by August Comte (1798-1857) indicating a philosophy of strict empiricism—the only genuine or legitimate knowledge claims are those founded directly on experience. Comte sought to advance the project of 'positive knowledge' by distinguishing this kind of dependable empirical knowledge from claims made by theology and *metaphysics*. He divided history into three stages—the theological, the metaphysical, and the positive. In the last stage, metaphysical speculation is dissolved by science. He developed a unified hierarchical conception of the sciences and argued that the goal of science was prediction accomplished by identifying laws of succession. Sociology, in his view, should aim at identifying the laws that govern the development of society. **See also** EMPIRICISM, LOGICAL EMPIRICISM, LOGICAL POSITIVISM.

POSTEMPIRICISM   This is the name for a collection of ideas and arguments that followed the demise of strict *empiricism*. The central claims of the postempiricist view are: (1) data are not detachable from theory; (2) the language of science is irreducibly metaphorical and inexact; (3) meanings are not separate from facts but determine facts; (4) scientific theories can never be either conclusively verified or conclusively refuted by data alone; (5) science consists of research projects or programs structured by presuppositions about the nature of reality. These claims are roughly equivalent to the contemporary understanding of the philosophy of science. Ironically, many contemporary defenders of 'qualitative' approaches to inquiry do not attack this postempiricist epistemology but a long-since-abandoned strict empiricism. For a full account of the postempiricist view, see H. I. Brown, *Perception, Theory and Commitment*, Univ. of Chicago Press, 1977; M. Hesse, *Revolutions and Reconstructions in the Philosophy of Science*, Indiana Univ. Press, 1980; A. O'Hear, *An Introduction to the Philosophy of Science*, Oxford, 1989; for a critique of a postempiricist account of research in an applied field, see W. Carr, *For Education: Toward Critical Educational Inquiry*, Open Univ. Press, 1995.

POSTMODERN ETHNOGRAPHY   See CRITICAL ETHNOGRAPHY, PARTICIPANT OBSERVATION, THICK DESCRIPTION.

P

POSTMODERNISM   Although this term and *poststructuralism* are often used interchangeably, postmodern theory or postmodernism is generally regarded as a more encompassing notion. Few scholars agree, however, as to what exactly the term means except perhaps that it represents a reaction to, critique of, or departure from 'modernism,' to which the Enlightenment gave birth. (And, of course, what is modernism is a matter of much dispute as well; see the discussion of modernity and postmodernity in David Harvey, *The Condition of Postmodernity*, Basil Blackwell, 1989.) The term originated as a description of a particular architectural style opposed to modernist architecture and eventually was applied to graphic arts, literature, and the contours of social and political life. It is radically interdisciplinary in character and rejects conventional styles of academic discourse. Postmodernism is an attitude toward the social world, more of a diagnosis than a theory. It opposes four central doctrines that form the core of the Enlightenment tradition: (1) the notion of a rational, autonomous subject; a self that has an essential human nature; (2) the notion of *foundationalist epistemology* (and foundationalist philosophy in general); (3) the notion of reason as a universal, a priori capacity of individuals; (4) the belief in social and moral progress through the rational application of social scientific theories to the arts and social institutions (law, family, education, and so on). Postmodernism is also characterized by its distrust of and incredulity toward all 'totalizing' discourses or metanarratives—those large-scale or grand theoretical frameworks that purportedly explain culture, society, human agency, and the like (see Jean-François Lyotard, *The Postmodern Condition—A Report on Knowledge*, Univ. of Minnesota Press, 1984). In place of these metaframeworks, postmodern theory endorses heterogeneity, difference, fragmentation, and indeterminacy. Postmodernism has its antecedents in the critiques of modernity provided by Friedrich Nietzsche (1844-1900) and Martin Heidegger (1889-1976) and is championed by French social theorists Jean-François Lyotard, Michel Foucault, Jean Baudrillard, Gilles Deleuze, and Félix Guattari (see the discussion of these theorists in Steven Best and Douglas Kellner, *Postmodern Theory*, Guilford, 1991). It is also prominently debated among American scholars including the literary critic Fredric Jameson, sociologist Daniel Bell, and the feminist Nancy Fraser. Not all scholars associated with postmodern thought, however, describe their work as postmodern or themselves as postmodernists. For illustrations of the intellectual approach of postmodernism in social science generally see Pauline Rosenau, *Postmodernism and the Social Sciences*, Princeton Univ. Press, 1992; in sociology, see David R. Dickens and Andrea Fontana, eds., *Postmodernism and Social Inquiry*, Guilford, 1994; in anthropology, see George E. Marcus and Michael M. J. Fischer, *Anthropology as Cultural Critique*, Univ. of Chicago Press, 1986; in feminist theory, see Jane Flax, *Thinking Fragments*, Univ. of California Press, 1990; for a brief summary of the debates between critical theory and postmodern theory, see Steven Best and Douglas Kellner, *Postmodern Theory*, Guilford, 1991. **See also** CRISIS OF REPRESENTATION.

POSTPOSITIVISM   The term describes an attitude toward knowledge evident after the demise of epistemologies of science associated with *logical positivism* and *logical empiricism*—philosophies that sought to establish the foundation for all knowledge in sense experience. Broadly speaking, positivists were confident that sense experience (expressible as basic observation sentences or 'protocol statements') would guarantee the truth of scientific knowledge claims. Postpositivists accept that empirical observations are important but reject the idea that such observations provide an immutable foundation for knowledge claims. (They also reject the claims of rationalists that reason provides an immutable foundation.) Postpositivists argue that the best we can do is develop contingent, fallible knowledge claims. There is great variation in postpositivist views of the aim of social inquiry, the role of method, and so forth. Constructivist, feminist, poststructural, phenomenological, hermeneutic, critical social science, and *postempiricist* approaches to inquiry are all postpositivist in the sense of the term defined here. The term at best is an overarching designation for all efforts undertaken since the demise of logical empiricism in the 1950s to develop philosophies and methodologies for social and natural science.

POSTSTRUCTURALISM   A critique of *structuralism* that arose in the early 1970s and was principally authored by the French scholars Jacques Derrida, Michel Foucault, Julia Kristeva, Jean-François Lyotard, and Roland Barthes. It is resolutely antiempirical, antimetaphysical, antihumanist, antirationalist and literary in its inception. Although there is much variation among the views of the cluster of scholars identified as poststructuralist, several central themes are identifiable (see S. Best and D. Kellner, *Postmodern Theory*, Guilford, 1991; A. Giddens, "Structuralism, Poststructuralism, and the Production of Culture," in A. Giddens and J. H. Turner, eds., *Social Theory Today*, Stanford Univ. Press, 1987; P. Rosenau, *Postmodernism and the Social Sciences*, Princeton Univ. Press, 1992): (1) The decentering of the notion of an individual, self-aware condition of being a subject. Poststructuralists question the value and existence of the metaphysical notion of a human being or conscious subject as a datum. The 'I' is not immediately available to itself because it derives its identity only from its position in language or its involvement in various systems of signification. Hence, subjects, authors, and speakers are irrelevant to the interpretation of texts. (2) Pantextualism—everything is a *text*—and all texts are interrelated, which makes for 'intertextuality.' (3) Meaning is unstable, never fixed, never determined or determinate, never representational. Here, poststructuralists reverse a conventional structuralist *semiotic* understanding. In Saussere's structuralism, a sign (e.g., 'chair') links a signifier (a perceptible image) and a signified (a concept, e.g., 'a piece of furniture on which to sit'). Perceptible images are thought to come to rest in the concepts of a conscious mind. But for poststructuralists, the meaning of a sign is never produced in this kind of stable, referential relationship. Rather, the signified is but an instant in a never-ending process of continuous signification; an infinite referral of signifier to signified. The sign has an arbitrary nature; this leads to an infinite play of meaning. (4) *Deconstructionism* is a poststructuralist strategy for reading texts that unmasks the supposed 'truth' or meaning of text by undoing, reversing, and displacing taken-for-granted binary oppositions that structure texts (e.g., right over wrong, subject over object, reason over nature, men over women, speech over writing, reality over appearance, and so forth). The following observation by the anthropologist Micaela di Leonardo briefly sums up the aims of poststructuralism: "Poststructuralist arguments [if that is the right word], by their very nature attempt to destabilize received conceptions of science, order, society, and the self. Poststructuralism is antiscience, antitheory; it levels our distinctions among truth and falsehood, science and myth. It denies the existence of social order or real human selves, declaring the death of the subject. ... [It] entails ... a 'logic of disintegration.' " ("Introduction: Gender, Culture, and Political Economy," in M. di Leonardo, ed., *Gender at the Crossroads of Knowledge: Feminist Anthropology in the Postmodern Era*, Univ. of California Press, 1991, p. 24). **See also** SEMIOTICS, STRUCTURALISM.

PRACTICAL-MORAL KNOWLEDGE   See PARADIGMATIC KNOWLEDGE CLAIM, PRAXIS.

PRACTICE See PRAXIS.

PRAGMATISM   Perhaps the only uniquely American philosophy, pragmatism is best known through the work of William James (1842-1910), John Dewey (1859-1952), and Charles Sanders Peirce (1839-1914), and its current revival as neopragmatism in the works of Richard Rorty. For a historical overview of the contributions of key pragmatic philosophers, compare H. S. Thayer, *Meaning and Action: A Critical History of Pragmatism*, 2nd ed., Hacksett, 1981, and C. West, *The American Evasion of Philosophy: A Genealogy of Pragmatism*, Univ. of Wisconsin Press, 1989. There are many versions of pragmatism and some are radically different, for example, the pragmatism of Peirce and that of Rorty. But, broadly speaking, this philosophy views knowledge as an instrument or tool for organizing experience and it is deeply concerned with the union of theory and practice. For qualitative inquiry, pragmatism or the pragmatic outlook is important for at least two reasons: (1) Pragmatism is a philosophical source of *symbolic interactionism* and the *Chicago School* of sociology (see, for example, H. Joas, *Pragmatism and Social Theory*, Univ. of Chicago Press, 1993; H. Joas, "Symbolic Interactionism," in *Social Theory Today*, A. Giddens and J. Turner, eds., Stanford Univ. Press, 1987; N. K. Denzin, *Symbolic Interactionism and Cultural Studies*, Blackwell, 1992). (2) The contemporary pragmatic outlook comprises a set of ideas that are often appealed to in defending qualitative inquiry as a viable option in the social sciences. Richard J. Bernstein (*The New Constellation: The Ethical-Political Horizons of Modernity/Postmodernity*, MIT Press, 1991, p. 326ff.) identifies these substantive themes as (1) antifoundationalism; (2) a "thoroughgoing fallibilism in which we realize that although we must begin any inquiry with prejudgments and can never call everything into question at once, nevertheless there is no belief or thesis—no matter how fundamental—that is not open to further interpretation and criticism"; (3) "the social character of the self and the need to cultivate a critical community of inquirers"; (4) an "awareness and sensitivity to radical contingency and chance that mark the universe, our inquiries, our lives"; (5) the view that there can be no escape from the plurality of traditions, perspectives, and philosophic orientations. For a critique of pragmatism, see J. Diggins, *The Promise of Pragmatism: Modernism and the Crisis of Knowledge and Authority,* Univ. of Chicago, 1994. **See also FALLIBILISM.**

PRAXIS   This is a term for a particular form of human activity that means something different from our common usage of the word 'practice.' To understand this difference, we must consider how Aristotle (*Nicomachean Ethics,* Book VI) contrasted praxis with *poiesis.* Wilfred Carr ("What is an Educational Practice?" in Carr, *For Education: Toward a Critical Educational Theory,* Open Univ. Press, 1995) explains the distinction as follows: *Poiesis* is a kind of making or instrumental action. It has an end in view or an object in mind prior to any action. It is activity that brings about specific products, and it requires a kind of technical know-how or expertise (*technē*). Praxis is also directed at a specific end but its aim is not to produce an object but to realize some morally worthwhile good: "The 'good' for the sake of which a practice [praxis] is pursued cannot be 'made,' it can only be 'done.' 'Practice' is a form of 'doing action' precisely because its end can only be realized through action and can only exist in the action itself" (p. 68). Furthermore, the ends of praxis are not immutable or fixed but are constantly revised as the goods internal to a practice are pursued.

Conceived in this way, praxis is not defined in opposition to *theory,* as we commonly do today. Often we hear that theory is nonpractical and practice is nontheoretical. Theory is something 'applied to' practice, or practice is the domain in which scientific theory is 'used.' Theory is about knowledge, practice about action; theory is thinking, practice is doing. Aristotle (*Nicomachean Ethics,* Book I.vi.11ff., 1096a-1097a) wrote: "The same exactitude is not to be looked for in all fields of knowledge, any more than in all kinds of crafts. It is the mark of an educated mind to expect just that exactitude in any subject that the nature of the matter permits. For it is unreasonable to accept merely plausible arguments from a mathematician, and to demand formal demonstrations from an orator." Aristotle was interested in exploring different fields of knowledge, the problems unique to each, and the kinds of reasoning appropriate to solving those problems. He viewed theoretical science and practical science as two different forms of human activity each with its own particular kind of knowledge, intellectual virtues, commitments, purposes, and ethical demands. The goal of theoretical science is the production of theoretical or scientific knowledge (*episteme*). This kind of knowledge requires the contemplative disposition of the philosopher or scientist. The knowledge sought through this kind of activity is characterized by the activities of proof, demonstration, and analytical reasoning, and the knowledge is expressible in timeless, necessary, universal propositions. What is known 'scientifically' holds true generally.

Practical science, in contrast, has a different goal and requires a different kind of theorizing or reasoning. It demands an intellectual and moral disposition toward right living and the pursuit of human good and hence a form of reasoning and knowledge that is practical-moral (*phronesis*). *Phronesis* is intimately concerned with the timely, the local, the particular and the contingent. It involves a distinctive way of relating the particular, and the general that is distinct from the effort in theoretical knowledge to subsume all particular cases under a general rule, principle, or law. In theoretical science, knowledge of the general is more important than knowledge of the particular. We understand the latter in terms of the former. In practical knowledge, this relation is reversed: Knowledge of the particular is primary, and we understand the general only in light of the contingent features of the case at hand.

Some of the strongest criticisms of social science in recent decades have been directed at the connection between social science and instrumental control and technical mastery of the social world and at the tendency of social scientists to assimilate all practical problems of social life to technical solutions. This theme echoes throughout critical, feminist, hermeneutic, and postmodern perspectives. It is a concern in all fields in which social science investigations hold court including education, health care, management, and psychotherapy. One alternative to the technicist picture of the purpose and use of social science is this conception of practical knowledge or practical wisdom that has its roots in Aristotle. This is a widespread development in philosophy (see, for example, J. Dunne, *Back to the Rough Ground: 'Phronesis' and 'Technē' in Modern Philosophy and in Aristotle*, Univ. of Notre Dame Press, 1993; A. R. Jonsen and S. Toulmin, *The Abuse of Casuistry*, Univ. of California Press, 1988; A. MacIntyre, *After Virtue*, Univ. of Notre Dame Press, 1981) that is making its way into social science thinking about qualitative inquiry. Recovery and elaboration of the concept of praxis and of the relation of theory to praxis is important for qualitative inquiry: Aristotelian ideas about praxis and practical-moral knowledge are central to the ***philosophical hermeneutics*** of Hans-Georg Gadamer and Charles Taylor (see, for example, H.-G. Gadamer, *Reason in the Age of Science*, trans. F. G. Lawrence, MIT Press, 1981; C. Taylor, *Philosophical Papers, Vol. 2*, Cambridge Univ. Press, 1985; see also the discussion of Gadamer's views in R. J. Bernstein, *Beyond Objectivism and Relativism*, Univ. of Pennsylvania Press, 1983). And the distinction between *technē* and *phronesis* figures prominently in Jürgen Habermas's critical theory of society (*Knowledge and Human Interests*, trans. J. J. Shapiro, Beacon, 1971; *The Theory of Communicative Action, Vol. 1*, trans. T. McCarthy, Beacon, 1981). **See also PARADIGMATIC KNOWLEDGE CLAIM.**

(THE) PROBLEM OF CRITERIA   The central project of *epistemology* is the justification of knowledge claims—how are we to decide that any particular account or interpretation of the world is valid, genuine, legitimate, true? Philosophers and methodologists have devoted much effort to specifying the appropriate *criteria* for making such an assessment. The legitimization of social scientific inquiry has hinged on the fact that it is particularly preoccupied with means for developing and testing accounts of social phenomena for their accuracy or truth. The advent of ***postmodernism*** and ***poststructuralism*** in social thought has cast the project of epistemological justification and hence the traditional grounds of authority for social science into question. For some scholars issues of epistemological criteria no longer matter, what does matter is political justification. For other scholars the epistemological and the political are collapsed into an interlocking larger issue. Of course, social science has always had scholars who focused on the political nature of the enterprise. But within recent decades, concerns about the politics of method, hostility toward authoritative claims of *representation,* denials of the possibility of truth, and so forth have called into question the importance of the search for *epistemic criteria* in social science. For many social theorists, the central problem of social science is no longer one of developing the best criteria for establishing genuine knowledge but rather one of unmasking the values and politics of the enterprise of social inquiry that were hidden within the epistemological project. **See also CRISIS OF REPRESENTATION, EPISTEMOLOGY, VALIDITY.**

PROPOSITIONAL KNOWLEDGE   On a relatively commonsense interpretation, propositions are sentences or statements that express in written or spoken language what we believe, doubt, affirm, or deny. (Of course we express these dispositions in other ways as well.) Assertions, interpretations, evaluations, conclusions, findings, hypotheses, and the like are familiar kinds of propositions or statements.

Propositional knowledge is knowing-that; an assertion <u>that</u> something is so. It is a kind of knowledge distinguishable from knowing how; knowledge of how to do something. The phrase "propositional knowledge" is often used in the literature on qualitative inquiry in a way that connotes something more like abstract formal language. Logic is such a language, its grammar and interpretation are determined solely by rules defining its symbols. Propositional knowledge thus often means something like the expression of scientific knowledge claims in a formal mathematical calculus. (A propositional calculus employs symbols for variables in combination with logical operators also expressed in symbolic form, for example, $p \supset q$ is read "if p then q" or "p implies q"; $p \equiv q$ is read "p is equivalent to q" or "p if and only if q.") The logical positivists argued that all genuine scientific knowledge should be capable of expression in this kind of formal language. They believed that by stating (and analyzing) claims about the world using the tools of formal logic, one could arrive at a way of expressing knowledge claims in propositions that were unambiguous, timeless, and expres-

P

sive of unchanging relations. Qualitative inquiry in general opposes this view. Hence, when the phrase "propositional knowledge" is used in contrast to notions like tacit knowledge, experiential knowledge, practical knowledge, and so forth it may be a way of expressing opposition to the idea that there is only one way to speak of what constitutes genuine, legitimate knowledge of the world. **See also** NARRATIVE EPISTEMOLOGY, TACIT (PERSONAL) KNOWLEDGE.

PURPOSEFUL SAMPLING   The site in which a fieldworker chooses to study, or the case that he or she chooses to study, is often selected purposefully rather than on the basis of some random selection procedure. Sites or cases are chosen because there may be good reason to believe that 'what goes on there' is critical to understanding some process or concept, or to testing or elaborating some established theory. The site or case may also be chosen on the basis of prior knowledge that it is extreme, typical, deviant, unique, particularly revelatory, and so on. In all of these situations, the procedure for the selection of a site or case requires that the inquirer first establish some relevant criterion (criteria) and then choose a site or case because it meets that criterion (criteria). The logic of a criterion-based or purposeful selection procedure differs from a random selection procedure. In the latter, some population of sites or cases is defined and enumerated and the site or case is chosen from within that population using a procedure that ensures that all cases have an equal or known probability of being selected. **See also** SAMPLING.

P

QUALITATIVE This is a not-so-descriptive adjective attached to the varieties of social inquiry that have their intellectual roots in *hermeneutics, phenomenological sociology,* and the *Verstehen* tradition. Most scholars use the phrase 'qualitative inquiry' as a blanket designation for all forms of such inquiry including *ethnography, case study research, naturalistic inquiry, ethnomethodology, life history methodology, narrative inquiry,* and the like. It has been used as a modifier for the terms "data," "method," "methodology," "research," and "paradigm" and as a synonym for "nonexperimental" and "ethnographic." Because the adjective does not clearly signal a particular meaning, a great number and variety of scholars have attempted to define just what is the so-called qualitative paradigm, what are the basic characteristics of qualitative research, and so on. One might reasonably view the entire *Handbook of Qualitative Research* (Sage, 1994) as an attempt at an extended definition of the

Q

term. "Qualitative research" is simply not a very useful term for denoting a specific set of characteristics of inquiry.

Often, attempts at definition involve both implicit and explicit comparisons to the equally ambiguously used adjective 'quantitative.' Perhaps the clearest use of the adjective is to distinguish between qualitative data—nonnumeric data in the form of words—and quantitative data—numeric data. The earliest qualitative versus quantitative debates might better have been called "The Merits of Nonnumeric Versus Numeric Data Debates," but that doesn't have quite the same ring to it as the more common designation of the controversy. The same debate also meant defending as reliable and valid methods used to generate qualitative data (i.e., unstructured open-ended interviews, participant observation, and so on) from attacks by defenders of methods used to generate quantitative data (questionnaires, psychometric measures, tests, and so on).

'Qualitative' denotes of or relating to quality, and a quality, in turn, is an inherent or phenomenal property or essential characteristic of some thing (object or experience). Ironically, there appears to be only one variety of qualitative inquiry that takes the definition of quality as its starting point. Elliot Eisner's (e.g., *The Enlightened Eye*, Macmillan, 1991) explication of qualitative inquiry begins from the point of view that inquiry is a matter of the perception of qualities and an appraisal of their value. The work of Eisner and his students aims to define and illustrate an aesthetics that explains how qualitative aspects of the experiences and settings of teaching and learning are to be perceived, appreciated, interpreted, understood, and criticized. The metaphors he employs for capturing the dual features of his methodology are connoisseurship and criticism. **See also** FIELD STUDIES, QUANTITATIVE.

QUALITATIVE EVALUATION   A broad designation for a variety of approaches to evaluating (i.e., determining the merit or worth of, or both) social and educational programs, policies, projects, and technologies that make use of typically 'qualitative' methods for generating data (e.g., unstructured *interviewing, observation, document analysis*) and nonstatistical means of analyzing and interpreting that data. These approaches arose in the mid 1970s as a reaction to the dominance in evaluation practice of randomized and quasi-experimental designs and standardized measures of achievement. Included here are approaches known as case study evaluations (B. MacDonald and R. Walker, *Case Studies and the Social Philosophy of Educational Research,* Univ. of East Anglia, CARE, 1974); responsive evaluation (R. Stake, *Evaluating the Arts in Education: A Responsive Approach,* Charles E. Merrill, 1975); illuminative evaluation (D. Hamilton, *Beyond the Numbers Game,* Macmillan, 1977); and *naturalistic inquiry* or fourth-generation evaluation (E. Guba and Y. S. Lincoln, *Fourth Generation Evaluation,* Sage, 1989). A comprehensive review of these approaches and qualitative methods in evaluation is provided in M. Q. Patton, *Qualitative Evaluation and Research Methods,* 2nd ed., Sage, 1990.

QUANTITATIVE   An adjective indicating that something is expressible in terms of quantity, that is, a definite amount or number. Thus it is accurate to talk of quantitative measures and quantitative data. The term is often used, however, as a synonym for any design (e.g., experimental, survey) or procedure (e.g., statistical) that relies principally on the use of quantitative data and then contrasted with 'qualitative' accordingly. So-called 'qualitative' studies often can and do, however, make use of quantitative data. **See also** QUALITATIVE.

Q

RATIONAL CHOICE EXPLANATION. See EXPLANATION.

RATIONALISM A philosophical position composed of many variations that generally holds that reason is the primary way we acquire
knowledge. This view is opposed to *empiricism,* which privileges
sense experience as the basis for all knowledge. In the philosophy of
social science, Karl Popper's (1902-1994) critical rationalism is a
strong critique of the strict empiricism of *logical positivism.* The
great rationalist philosophers include Descartes (1596-1650), Kant
(1724-1804), and Leibniz (1646-1716). The rationalist argues that
minds have a priori structures or categories of understanding
that organize and give meaning to our sense experiences. For the
rationalist, data are neither the primary source of knowledge nor the
final arbiter of what constitutes a legitimate knowledge claim. For

several reasons, a basic understanding of rationalism is important for grasping the significance of qualitative inquiry: *constructivism* is a rationalist approach; *postmodernism* tends to reject both empiricism and rationalism; *philosophical hermeneutics* proposes a way of engaging the world that is significantly at odds with the detached or disinterested mode of engagement (i.e., a subject who stands apart from the object that he or she seeks to understand) characteristic of both empiricism and rationalism.

REALISM   This is the doctrine that there are real objects that exist independently of our knowledge of their existence. Scientific realism is the view that theories refer to real features of the world. 'Reality' here refers to whatever it is in the universe (i.e., forces, structures, and so on) that causes the phenomena that we perceive with our senses.

The relationship between *logical positivism* and realism can be a slippery one. The logical positivists believed that what is 'real' is a world of discrete or particular events that are observable. These events actually exist whether we observe them or not. But the interest of logical positivism in questions of 'reality' stopped there. They argued that the only sure path to knowing this world was the experience of the senses. Logical positivists were thoroughgoing empiricists. They believed that reality is that which can be observed and what we can observe are only the constant conjunction of events—some set of events is followed by the appearance of events of another kind. 'Explanations' are thus simply a question of locating an event to be explained in (i.e., 'covering it' with) an observed regularity. For the logical positivist, there is nothing 'deeper,' so to speak, to the notion of explanation than the proper logical arrangement of well-verified observations. The test of whether a theory is 'true' or 'false' is nothing more than a test of its success or failure at predicting events. Hence, there is no need to talk of whether theories actually refer to 'real' causes, forces, necessities, mechanisms, or any other such unobservable 'real' underlying entities. All such talk is metaphysical speculation and has no place in what constitutes genuine, legitimate scientific knowledge. Logical positivists did not deny that there was a 'real' world; they insisted that the world consists of

R

observable particulars. But they rejected any elements of realism in their *epistemology* (i.e., in their theories of what constituted a legitimate scientific explanation).

Scientific realism argues that what is 'real' is not necessarily only that which we can directly observe. It agrees with logical positivism that there is a world of events 'out there' and that there are patterns or regularities of events that can be observed. Scientific realists, however, distinguish the 'empirical' (that which we observe with our senses) from the 'real' (the processes that generate the events we observe). Realism rejects logical positivist epistemology. It holds that to claim genuine, scientific knowledge it is important to decide whether theories are 'really' true or false (and not just valid by virtue of their ability to predict), whether something like a 'cause' really exists, whether there really are things 'out there' like electrons, gravity, force fields, society, social structures, and the like. Realists believe that a genuine scientific 'explanation' must 'go beyond' statements of observed regularities to get at the mechanisms, processes, structures, or whatever unobservable, 'real,' underlying forces actually account for the regularities (constant conjunctions) that we observe. Postempiricist notions of scientific realism are complicated philosophical doctrines (see, for example, F. Suppe, ed., *The Structure of Scientific Theories*, 2nd ed., Univ. of Illinois Press, 1977; R. Bashkar, *A Realist Theory of Science*, Leeds Books, 1975; W. Outhwaite, *New Philosophies of Social Science: Realism, Hermeneutics, and Critical Theory*, St. Martin's, 1987; J. K. Smith, *After the Demise of Empiricism*, Ablex, 1993).

The relationship between qualitative methodologies and realism is equally complex and slippery. Although some versions of *constructivism* do appear to deny an external reality, many (if not most, I suspect) qualitative inquirers have a common-sense realist *ontology*, that is, they take seriously the existence of things, events, structures, people, meanings, and so forth in the environment as independent in some way from their experience with them. And they regard society, institutions, feelings, intelligence, poverty, disability, and so on as being just as 'real' as the toes on their feet and the sun in the sky. Hence, when we read that qualitative studies are somehow opposed to the doctrine of realism we must be careful to unpack the meaning of that objection. Some objections are directed at what is called naive realism—roughly, the view that the world as it appears to be to us is the world; it is captured in the phrase that knowledge is 'given' in experience, that is, it is <u>directly</u> perceived, and no intermediate mental state or subjective awareness exists between the perceiver and the object to be perceived. The naive realist assumes that scientific theories literally mirror reality. Other objections to realism are directed at its externalist or 'outsider' perspective on knowledge—a perspective associated with a separation of investigator and object of investigation, with 'representing' the world in social theories, and with the necessity of correspondence between concepts or theories and observations (see, for example, J. K. Smith, *The Nature of Social and Educational Inquiry*, Ablex, 1989, pp. 69ff). See also CONSTRUCTIVISM, EMPIRICISM, ETHNOGRAPHIC REALISM, IDEALISM, INSIDER/OUTSIDER PERSPECTIVE, OBJECTIVISM, REPRESENTATION.

REDUCTIONISM   This is the idea that we can (and ought to) replace one vocabulary by a second vocabulary that is more primary. Examples of attempts at reductionism include the logical positivists' bid to reduce the vocabulary of theory to the vocabulary of observation statements; logicism—the bid to reduce mathematics to logic; the reduction of psychology to neurology; the reduction of social science explanations to natural science explanations, especially those of physics. The phrase "the whole is more than the sum of its parts" often is uttered as an objection to reductionism by systems theorists who argue for the doctrine of holism and defenders of Gestalt psychology who object to the reductionist tendencies of associationist or behaviorist psychology. It is often said that defenders of qualitative inquiry endorse holism and oppose efforts at reductionism. Yet this may more likely be a defense of contextualism than holism—that is, an argument for the importance of understanding the meaning of particular language and *human action* in the specific context in which it unfolds. For a discussion of the various ways of understanding both holism and reductionism, see D. C. Phillips, *Holistic Thought in Social Science*, Stanford Univ. Press, 1976.

REFLEXIVITY   Also called reflectivity, this refers to two somewhat different ideas informing qualitative inquiry. (1) A traditional interpretation of reflexivity signals the process of critical self-reflection on one's biases, theoretical predispositions, preferences, and so forth. This kind of self-inspection can be salutary for any kind of inquiry, and fieldworkers are often encouraged to record and explore these evolving dispositions in personal notes in their *field journals*. (2) Reflexivity, however, also signals more than inspection of potential sources of bias and their control; it points to the fact that the inquirer is part of the setting, context, and social phenomenon he or she seeks to understand. Hence, reflexivity can be a means for critically inspecting the entire research process including (1) reflecting on what Roger Sanjek ("On Ethnographic Validity," in Sanjek, ed., *Fieldnotes*, Cornell Univ. Press, 1990) calls the ethnographer's path (the ways in which a fieldworker establishes a social network of informants and participants in a study); (2) examining one's personal and theoretical commitments to see how they serve as resources for generating particular data, for behaving in particular ways vis-à-vis respondents and participants, and for developing particular interpretations. Reflexivity is held to be a very important procedure for establishing the *validity* of accounts of social phenomena. This is particularly true for many critical researchers concerned with the charge that their research can become nothing more than a self-serving ideology (see, for example, J. Thomas, *Doing Critical Ethnography*, Sage, 1993) as well as for feminist researchers wary of duplicating androcentric perspectives and race and class bias in their investigations (see, for example, N. Scheper-Hughes, *Death Without Weeping*, Univ. of California Press, 1992; M. M. Fonow and J. A. Cook, eds., *Beyond Methodology: Feminist Scholarship as Lived Research*, Indiana Univ. Press, 1991). **See also BIAS, CRITICAL SOCIAL SCIENCE.**

RELATIVISM   In general, this is the doctrine that denies that there are universal truths. There are several ways in which the term is used: (1) as the opposite of the idea of *objectivism*. For example, Richard J. Bernstein (*Beyond Objectivism and Relativism*, Univ. of Pennsylvania Press, 1983, p. 8) defines relativism as the belief that notions of rationality, truth, goodness, rightness, and reality can <u>only</u> be understood as relative to some specific theoretical framework, language game, conceptual scheme, set of social practices, or culture. The fear of those who believe in objectivism is that unless we can find foundations for our knowledge, we are doomed to relativism and radical *skepticism.* (2) As descriptive cultural relativism: A long-standing perspective in anthropology, this is the view that acceptable social practices (or the morality of such practices) differ from society to society or culture to culture. Cultural relativists (those who simply describe differing social practices), however, are not necessarily ethical relativists (in the sense of relativism defined above): An ethical relativist holds that there are <u>no</u> universally valid moral principles. (3) As cognitive relativism: This is the view that there are no universal truths about the world. In this sense many social constructionists and poststructuralists are cognitive relativists. Furthermore, the cognitive relativism of *poststructuralism* is equivalent to what Friedrich Nietzsche (1844-1900) termed the interpretive and radically perspectival character of all knowing—there can be no such thing as absolute knowledge that transcends all perspectives; we must face the fact that there are only interpretations of interpretations.

Practically speaking, it seems unlikely that anyone could practice radical relativism—the view that any interpretation, value, and so forth is as good as any other; or, in a phrase, "anything goes." For to hold that relativism is <u>the</u> philosophical position is a contradiction in terms. Likewise, to hold the view that there are no final interpretations, only the infinite play of multiple interpretations, is no longer to be a relativist, for one is arguing that this is <u>the</u> way things are.

RELIABILITY   This is an *epistemic criterion* thought to be necessary but not sufficient for establishing the truth of an account or interpretation of a social phenomenon. An account is judged to be reliable if it is capable of being replicated by another inquirer. Traditionally, social scientists assume that although not all repeatable or replicable observations or accounts are necessarily valid, all valid accounts are (at least in principle) replicable. Opinion is divided among qualitative researchers over whether this criterion has any meaning whatsoever in judging the accuracy of fieldwork accounts. Jerome Kirk and Marc Miller (*Reliability and Validity in Qualitative Research*, Sage, 1986) emphasize the importance of repeatability of observations within a given study both diachronically (the stability of a fieldworker's observations across data drawn from different time periods) and synchronically (similar observations within the same time period across different methods, e.g., observation and interview). The sociologist David Silverman (*Interpreting Qualitative Data*, Sage, 1993) endorses a similar view and argues that reliability can and must be addressed in fieldwork by such procedures as using conventionalized methods for recording fieldnotes and analyzing transcripts, as well as making interrater checks on coding and categorization procedures and results. In their discussion of **trustworthiness criteria,** Yvonna Lincoln and Egon Guba (*Naturalistic Inquiry*, Sage, 1985) called for the importance of establishing **dependability**—an analog to reliability—through careful documentation of procedures for generating and interpreting data. Yet, the anthropologist Roger Sanjek ("On Ethnographic Validity," in R. Sanjek, ed., *Fieldnotes*, Cornell Univ. Press, 1990, p. 394) argues that "in ethnography, 'reliability' verges on affectation. We cannot expect and do not hope that another investigator will repeat the fieldwork and confirm the results." He represents the view that ethnographic fieldwork is principally preoccupied with **validity** (accurate descriptions of **human action**) and that this can be established without recourse to establishing the replicability of the account.

REPRESENTATION   Depicting, portraying, or describing social phenomena is a goal not simply of qualitative inquiry but of all forms of social science. Representation in its many forms—as resemblance, replication, repetition, description, duplication, and so forth—is central to the modernist project of understanding the world (P. Rosenau, *Postmodernism and the Social Sciences*, Princeton Univ. Press, 1992). But whether inquirers ought to claim that they 'represent' the social world in their studies and precisely what they are doing when they try to represent is a matter of great dispute. Few social inquirers any longer cling to naive **realism** and argue that their accounts are a literal mirror or representation of an external reality, yet few would also abandon the idea that their portrayals, depictions, or descriptions although fictions (in the sense of invented or crafted), should not also be accurate. Many struggle with the idea of fallible representation—seeking to find ways to give evidence or good reasons for their accounts that represent social phenomena without claiming that those accounts are certain or beyond revision. Many postmodernists find the idea of representation reprehensible.

They argue that representation assumes *objectivism* and that the goal of *deconstructionism* is to reveal the foolishness of all representational claims. Rosenau (pp. 94-95) sums up the radical postmodernist view: "representation is politically, socially, culturally, linguistically, and epistemologically arbitrary. It signifies mastery. . . . It signals distortion; it assumes unconscious rules governing relationships. It concretizes, finalizes, and excludes complexity. . . . [It] is fraudulent, perverse, artificial, mechanical, deceptive, incomplete, misleading, insufficient, wholly inadequate for the postmodern age." For these postmodernists, there is no such thing as the 'original' of anything that stands in some relation of equivalence to its representation; there is only the endless play of different meanings. Whether or not one accepts this radical diagnosis, the issue of representation in qualitative studies is highly problematic and contested. **See also** CRISIS OF REPRESENTATION, VALIDITY.

RESPONDENT   This is a common label designating the individual(s) who provide information (through interviews, conversations, and so on) in qualitative studies. Because of the negative connotations of the term 'subject' (in an experimental study or survey, for example), many qualitative inquirers have sought a less offensive term. Respondent, participant, and informant are all alternatives, although each carries a somewhat different meaning and is typically associated with a particular approach to qualitative work. For example, ethnographers usually speak of informants, action researchers refer to participants in a study, and so on. **See also** KEY INFORMANT.

RESPONDENT VALIDATION   See MEMBER CHECK.

R

SAMPLING   There are two important sampling issues in qualitative studies: <u>selecting</u> a field site in which to study some phenomenon (or developing a *case* through which to study some phenomenon) and <u>sampling within</u> the case or field site. Generally, following the advice of Clifford Geertz, we can say that the locus of a study (i.e., where one studies) is not the object of the study (i.e., what one studies). The fieldworker does not study <u>a</u> place or site (school, community, group, organization, and so on) but investigates some phenomenon (social process, *human action*) <u>within</u> a place or site. The selection of a site—school, classroom, homeless shelter, family, emergency room, and so on—(or the definition of a case) is generally not made on the basis of a random sampling procedure designed to yield a representative site. The logic of probability sampling is rarely applied in site selection. Rather, the site or place (or person) is chosen on the basis of a combination of criteria including availability, acces-

S

sibility, and theoretical interest. A <u>single</u> place may be chosen because in that site one has good reasons to believe that (1) the human action or social process going on there (e.g., marrying, negotiating, teaching, healing, working, gift-giving) is critical to understanding, testing, or elaborating on some theory or generalized concept of that social process, or (2) the social process unfolding there is extreme, deviant, or unique, or (3) the site or case is particularly revelatory or previously inaccessible. <u>Multiple</u> places, cases, or sites for study are chosen to facilitate comparisons either because they are likely to yield predictable contrasts in understanding the definition of social action or because they are likely to show the same or similar definition of social action (see, for example, M. Q. Patton, *Qualitative Evaluation and Research Methods*, 2nd ed., Sage, 1990; R. C. Yin, *Case Study Research*, rev. ed., Sage, 1989). Site or case selection is thus guided by the assumption that the study of the particular will shed some light on the general; study of a particular set of circumstances offers commentary on more than itself. This is why Clifford Geertz ("Thick Description: Toward an Interpretive Theory of Culture," in Geertz, *The Interpretation of Cultures*, Basic Books, 1973) can claim that "where an interpretation comes from does not determine where it can be compelled to go."

All sites or cases chosen for study must be carefully described relative to the nature of social action under investigation. This is necessary to document what the site is representative of; to answer the question "What is this a case of?" To create this kind of description, it is inadequate to offer only the standard litany of statistical-demographic data for a site (e.g., number of participants, age, gender, and so on) coupled with the usual physical description and geographical data (e.g., "a 200-bed hospital built in 1967 located in the rural midwest"). The kind of detail included in the description must provide readers with a sense of the typical acts, actions, relationships, and so on in the site. For example, Norman Denzin (*The Research Act*, 3rd ed., Prentice Hall, 1989) advises preparing representational maps that create a working picture of the temporal, ritual, and routine features of the persons, organizations, or social actions under study. Maps also pictorially display recurrent and stable features of the social phenomena under investigation. Without such a description, readers of a fieldwork report have no sound basis for comparing findings from the study in question to other similar social settings.

Within the place(s), site(s), or case(s) chosen for study a second set of sampling considerations becomes important. As one studies social action the concern should be something like "Is this usual or customary? Is this what typically goes on here, or is it being staged for my benefit?" To explore the nature and definition of social action within a particular site, the fieldworker considers sampling across time, occasions or events, and people. Representational maps also guide the selection of those specific events, activities, interactions, and so on that will be studied within the site. Imagine, for example, that a fieldworker has selected a court room as a profitable place in which to study the way in which lawyers and judges frame the behavior of juveniles charged with a crime. Before forming conclusions about the kinds of frames employed in that site, the fieldworker would want to be sure that he or she observed on several different occasions in court (mornings, afternoons, weekends, Mondays, Fridays, and so on), over several different events (complicated and uncomplicated cases), across several different types of plaintiffs (males and females, Caucasians, Hispanics, African Americans, and so on), and (if appropriate) several different kinds of lawyers and judges (experienced and inexperienced, male and female, and so on). This is what is meant by sampling within the site. See, for example, the discussion in M. Hammersley and P. Atkinson, *Ethnography: Principles in Practice*, Tavistock, 1983, pp. 45ff. **See also** CROSS-CASE ANALYSIS.

SCIENCE   One aspect of the contemporary debate about the academic status of qualitative inquiry into sociopolitical life is whether it can properly be called a science. In this regard, it is worth noting that the German term for "science" (*Wissenschaft*) has a much broader sense than that associated with the English use of the term "science," which is typically restricted to physics, chemistry, biology, and so forth. *Wissenschaft*, on the other hand, is not narrowly limited to those forms of science that employ the empirical methods of observation and experimentation, but refers to any systematic, rational form of inquiry with rigorous and intersubjectively agreed-on procedures for validation. *Wissenschaft* includes both the sciences of mathematics and logic and the hermeneutic and phenomenological disciplines concerned with the interpretation of meaning and the description of experience, respectively. The intellectual tradition encompassing all the methodological and epistemological concerns of the natural sciences is referred to as *Naturwissenschaften* and that tradition sets them apart from the tradition of the human or social sciences or *Geisteswissenschaften*. **Naturalism** is a defense of the former tradition, whereas **antinaturalism** defends the latter. Many poststructuralists would likely disavow any and all attempts to form something called a science of any kind, seeing such attempts as nothing more than linguistic inventions of totalizing, all-encompassing world views or metanarratives. See W. Outhwaite, *Understanding Social Life*, 2nd ed., Allen and Unwin, 1986, and the appendix in D. Polkinghorne, *Methodology for the Human Sciences*, SUNY Press, 1983 for a fuller discussion of the distinction between the two traditions. Edmund Husserl's (1859-1938) defense of phenomenology as a science is found in his *Phenomenology and the Crisis of Philosophy* (trans. Q. Lauer, Harper & Row, 1965). For a summary of postmodernist perspectives on science, see P. Rosenau, *Postmodernism and the Social Sciences*, Princeton Univ. Press, 1992. **See also** EXPLANATION, *VERSTEHEN*.

SCIENTISM   Jürgen Habermas (*Knowledge and Human Interests*, trans. J. J. Shapiro, Beacon, 1971, p. 4) provides this succinct definition: "Scientism means science's belief in itself: that is, the conviction that we can no longer understand science as one form of possible knowledge, but rather must identify knowledge with science." Scientism with respect to the social sciences can be equated with **naturalism,** with the belief that the explanatory aim and the requirements of method characteristic of natural science should govern the practice of social science. Scientism in philosophy is equivalent to the scientific philosophy of **logical positivism.** The term may have originated with F. A. Hayek (*The Counter-Revolution of Science: Studies in the Abuse of Reason*, 1955), who traced the idea to the French positivists Auguste Comte (1798-1857) and Henri Saint-Simon (1760-1825). In very general terms, twentieth-century Continental philosophy (e.g., phenomenology, existentialism, hermeneutics, critical theory, structuralism, deconstructionism) is characterized by its anti-scientism.

These philosophies offer a strong critique of what they regard as the devastating cultural and moral impact of scientism. In contrast, the analytic tradition in Anglo American philosophy has generally been much more science friendly (see, for example, D. E. Cooper, "Modern European Philosophy," in N. Bunnin and E. P. Tsui-James, eds., *The Blackwell Companion to Philosophy*, Blackwell, 1996). For a defense of moderate kind of scientism in social science see Scott Gordon, *The History and Philosophy of Social Science*, Routledge, 1991. For an historical examination of the rise of scientism in American social science see D. Ross, *The Origins of American Social Science*, Cambridge Univ. Press, 1991. **See also** NATURALISM.

SEMIOTICS   Also called semiology, this is the theory of signs or the theory investigating the relationship between knowledge and signs. A 'sign' is understood to be an entity or object that carries information, for example, a word, gesture, map, road sign, model, picture, diagram. A sign is a unity of signifier and signified. A signifier is an acoustic image of a spoken word as heard or read by a recipient of a vocal, written, or otherwise displayed message. The signified is the meaning called forth in the mind of the recipient resulting from the stimulation of the signifier. The major original contributors to this theory were the Swiss linguist Ferdinand de Saussure (1857-1913) and the American philosopher Charles Sanders Peirce (1839-1914). Saussure's work in structural linguistics is particularly significant for qualitative inquiry because it served as a major source for post-World War II French structuralism (popularized in the social anthropology of Lévi-Strauss). Structuralism, in turn, was the object of critique by interpretive anthropologists (e.g., Clifford Geertz), and structuralism shaped by Saussure's semiotic theory was the target of the poststructuralist criticisms of Jacques Derrida, Michel Foucault, Julia Kristeva, and Roland Barthes, among others. **See also** POST-STRUCTURALISM, STRUCTURALISM.

SENSITIZING CONCEPTS   A term coined by Herbert Blumer (*Symbolic Interactionism*, Prentice Hall, 1969) to refer to the way in which symbolic interactionists (and now qualitative inquirers more generally) make use of concepts in their research. Sociopsychological concepts like family, victim, stress, stigma, and so forth are held loosely at the outset of a study; they are not given full operational definitions so that the inquirer can explore how the concept is manifest in the particular set of circumstances under investigation. Sensitizing concepts are not *emic* or indigenous concepts but generated by the inquirer from existing studies and theory. They are used to provide a general sense of direction and reference for a study. Both Norman Denzin (*The Research Act*, 3rd ed., Prentice Hall, 1989) and Michael Patton (*Qualitative Evaluation and Research Methods*, 2nd ed., Sage, 1990) emphasize the importance of using a "sensitizing framework" at the outset of a qualitative study. The necessity of this kind of framework is further evidence of the impossibility of atheoretical research. **See also** THEORY.

SKEPTICISM   Radical skepticism argues that we can never know whether there is any knowledge (cognitive skepticism) or universally valid moral principles (ethical skepticism). More moderate versions of skepticism doubt that there is knowledge of certain kinds. A skeptical attitude characterizes the work of poststructuralists Michel Foucault and Jacques Derrida as well as the neopragmatism of Richard Rorty. **See also** RELATIVISM.

SOCIAL ACTION   See HUMAN ACTION.

SOCIAL CONSTRUCTIONISM   See CONSTRUCTIVISM.

STATISTICAL EXPLANATION   This is a form of causal explanation that seeks to complement evidence of statistical correlation with knowledge of causal factors or mechanisms through which observed correlations evolve. These explanations differ from *deductive-nomological explanations* only to the extent that they imply probabilistic as opposed to deterministic claims. These kinds of explanations are rare but not completely unknown in qualitative studies. A weak analog to this idea is found in the work in M. Miles and A. M. Huberman's *Qualitative Data Analysis*, 2nd ed., Sage, 1994. There they describe various means for developing empirically supportable causal networks, causal models, and causal chains linking variables. Although the associations between variables are not measured mathematically, the scheme reflects the underlying idea of establishing correlations among variables and developing a causal story explaining the mechanisms linking the variables into a network or chain. **See also** CAUSAL ANALYSIS, EXPLANATION.

STATISTICAL GENERALIZATION   See ANALYTIC GENERALIZATION.

STRUCTURALISM   This is both a way of thinking about the world and a methodology for investigating the world that is concerned with identifying and describing its underlying structures that cannot be observed but must be inferred. What exactly a structure is varies depending on the discipline in which structures are discussed; for example, the underlying determinate structure may be economic, as in the case of Marxism; a particular 'grammar' of language in the case of linguistics; a 'system' in system analysis; or gender relations in the case of some feminist structural analyses. Jean Piaget (1896-1980) (*Structuralism,* trans. and ed. C. Maschler, Routledge and Kegan Paul, 1971) provides a general definition of a structure as an arrangement of entities that are characterized by wholeness or internal coherence, dynamism, the capability of transforming or processing new material, and self-regulation. Structuralist theories descended from the work of the Swiss linguist Ferdinand Saussure (1857-1913) and the adaptation of Saussure's ideas for the analysis of language to the analysis of culture by the anthropologist Claude Lévi-Strauss in the 1960s. Roughly, Lévi-Strauss viewed aspects of cultural behavior—ceremonies, kinship relations, rites, totemic systems, marriage laws, myths, and so forth—not as entities in their own right but as structures in the larger whole or system called culture. Taken together these aspects form a kind of language and each aspect is a partial expression of the total language. The organization of culture becomes intelligible through an analysis of its relational structures in much the same way that the organization of a language is made clear by analyzing its grammar. Structuralism in anthropology is often criticized for its failure to consider the human or subjective side of culture. The interpretive anthropologist Clifford Geertz, for example, evaluated Lévi-Strauss' work as "aloof, closed, cold, airless, cerebral. . . . Neither picturing lives nor evoking them, neither interpreting them or explaining them, but rather arranging the materials the lives have somehow left behind into formal systems of correspondences" (*Works and Lives: The Anthropologist as Author,* Stanford Univ. Press, 1988, p. 48). Structuralist thinking spread beyond the boundaries of linguistics and anthropology to influence other disciplines including philosophy, literary theory, biology, physical anthropology, and political theory. Its central ideas of widespread structural regularities across time and space and its commitment to forming a scientific basis for the study of the innate properties of human nature, human cognition, language, and sociocultural phenomena found great appeal. For an overview of the theory, see T. Hawks, *Structuralism and Semiotics*, Univ. of California Press, 1977; A. Giddens, "Structuralism, Poststructuralism and the Production of Culture" in A. Giddens and J. H. Turner, eds., *Social Theory Today*, Stanford Univ. Press, 1987. **See also** FUNCTIONALISM, POSTSTRUCTURALISM.

SUBJECTIVE/SUBJECTIVITY Subjective can mean (1) the personal view of an individual; (2) unwarranted or unsupported (or unwarrantable, insupportable); and (3) biased or prejudiced. These three senses of the term are not necessarily equivalent. Just because a statement or claim is someone's personal view that does not therefore make it an unwarranted or biased view. Subjectivity is also often roughly equated with all that is normative and emotive (values, feelings, and so on), in contrast with all that is empirical and therefore objective (e.g., observation, fact, and so on).

Thomas Kuhn in *The Essential Tension* (Univ. of Chicago Press, 1977) sought to distinguish the judgmental character of a choice, decision, or statement from its subjective character. He argued that there are some kinds of subjective choices that are simply matters of taste, for example, when one expresses "I like ice cream." But when one is called on to make a personal judgment, then one must give reasons that support that judgment. To be rational and reasonable in this case is to give reasons for one's judgment.

Many postmodernists reject the language of subject and subjectivity altogether as being the trappings of modernity. They are postsubjective or champion the decline of subjectivity, which means they aim to deemphasize the subject as focus for analysis. They also seek to do away with the idea of a rational, unified subject as knower, arguing that there are multiple and contradictory subjectivities that are produced by discursive practices (see, for example, P. Rosenau, *Postmodernism and the Social Sciences*, Princeton Univ. Press, 1992, pp. 42-61). **See also** JUDGMENT, OBJECTIVE/OBJECTIVITY, SUBJECTIVISM.

SUBJECTIVISM   There are two different senses of this term: (1) First, the doctrine that holds that all judgments (claims, interpretations, assertions, and so forth) are <u>nothing but</u> reports of an individual speaker's feelings, attitudes, and beliefs, or that whatever one claims to be the case is nothing but a matter of personal opinion or taste. This understanding of subjectivism is compatible with radical *relativism,* that is, the view that 'anything goes.' (2) Second, it is the doctrine that holds that subjectivity is the ultimate reality, so to speak. Edmund Husserl's (1859-1938) phenomenology of transcendental subjectivism is a well-known example. Husserl offered two kinds of arguments against the doctrine of *realism:* He attempted to show that there is no real world that is wholly independent of the 'subject' that knows or experiences that world, and that the knowing subject does not itself belong to the world that it knows or experiences, that is, this subject is the "transcendental Ego" (see, for example, M. Hammond, J. Howarth, and R. Keat, *Understanding Phenomenology,* Blackwell, 1991). This understanding of subjectivism is clearly not equivalent to relativism because Husserl sought to show that transcendental subjectivity was a <u>universal</u> truth. **See also** OBJECTIVISM.

SYMBOLIC INTERACTIONISM   A social psychological and sociological theory with roots in American pragmatism. Like all frameworks informing qualitative studies, this theory comes in a variety of forms and thus is difficult to summarize briefly (for summaries and different varieties see N. K. Denzin, *Symbolic Interactionism and Cultural Studies,* Blackwell, 1992; H. Joas, "Symbolic Interactionism," in A. Giddens and J. H. Turner, eds., *Social Theory Today,* Stanford Univ. Press, 1987; K. Plummer, ed., *Symbolic Interactionism, Vols. 1 and 2: Classic and Contemporary Issues,* Edward Elgar, 1991). Many of the shared assumptions of this school of thought derive from the work of Herbert Blumer (*Symbolic Interactionism: Perspective and Method,* Prentice Hall, 1969), who, in turn, was influenced by the philosopher and social theorist George Herbert Mead (1863-1931). The Blumer-Mead version of symbolic interactionism rests on three premises: (1) Humans act toward the objects and people in their environment on the basis of the meanings these objects and people have for them. (2) These meanings derive from the social interaction (communication, broadly understood) between and among individuals. Communication is symbolic because we communicate through language and other symbols and in communicating create significant symbols. (3) Meanings are established and modified through an interpretive process undertaken by the individual actor. The influence of pragmatism on symbolic interactionism is evident in the latter's claim that humans are purposive agents who confront a world that must be interpreted rather than a world composed of a set of stimuli to which the individual must react. The meanings an actor forms in interpreting the world are instruments for guiding and forming action. Symbolic interactionism is thus characterized by its rejection of associationist or behaviorist psychologies. It also evinces a profound respect for the empirical world; to understand the process of meaning making, the inquirer must attend carefully to the overt behaviors, speech, and particular circumstances of behavior settings in which interaction takes place. The inquirer can understand human action only by first actively entering the setting or situation of the people being studied to see their particular definition of the situation, what they take into account, and how they interpret this information. For an overview of the perspective and its methodological principles, see N. K. Denzin, *The Research Act*, 3rd ed., Prentice Hall, 1989.

S

TACIT (PERSONAL) KNOWLEDGE   Tacit knowledge is having an awareness of certain things in a way that is quite different from focusing our attention on them. It is knowledge of particulars and something one can know and describe less precisely or more inarticulately than usual. In *Naturalistic Inquiry* (Sage, 1985) Yvonna Lincoln and Egon Guba argued that the tacit knowledge of the field researcher as 'human instrument' plays a significant role in distinguishing the methods of ***naturalistic inquiry*** from the methods of conventional social inquiry. Tacit knowledge enabled field researchers to be situationally responsive and to key into potentially important information. Lincoln and Guba claimed that this kind of adaptability and flexibility of the 'human instrument' that possessed tacit knowledge marked naturalistic inquiry as uniquely different from experimental and quasi-experimental inquiry that relied on paper-and-pencil instruments (i.e., questionnaires) and mechanical recording devices for data gathering.

Viewed more broadly, a defense of the importance (even necessity) of tacit or personal knowing in scientific inquiry plays a significant role in criticisms of *logical positivism* and *logical empiricism.*
These philosophies sought to eliminate from science (or at least
greatly minimize) tacit knowledge or, more broadly, any kind of knowing that would be regarded as personal *judgment* and appraisal that
might involve the emotions. This was to be accomplished by sepa-
rating the activities involved in formulating a hypothesis or problem
for investigation (context of discovery) from those activities required
in the testing of the hypothesis and the subsequent verification and
justification of a knowledge claim (context of justification). The
predilections, interests, and so on of the inquirer could play a role in
the first context but not in the second. Legitimate, genuine scientific
knowledge was regarded as impersonal, objective, and universally
established.

The chemist and philosopher Michael Polanyi (*Personal Knowledge: Toward a Postcritical Philosophy,* Univ. of Chicago Press, 1958) is
generally credited with explaining why this ideal of scientific detachment is suspect and pointing out that the personal participation
of the knower in all acts of knowing (including scientific knowing in
the context of justification) is essential. Polanyi argued that the
inevitable inclusion of personal, tacit assessments and judgments in
all aspects of knowledge acquisition did not necessarily undermine
the objectivity of science but rather called for an alternative analysis
of scientific objectivity. Polanyi summarized his argument as follows: "The processes of knowing (and so also of science) in no way
resemble an impersonal achievement of detached objectivity. They
are rooted throughout (from our selection of a problem to the verification of a discovery) in personal acts of tacit integration. They are
not grounded on explicit operations of logic. Scientific inquiry is
accordingly a dynamic exercise of the imagination and is rooted in
commitments and beliefs about the nature of things. It is a fiduciary
act. It is far from skepticism itself. It depends upon firm beliefs. . . .
Science is not thus the simon-pure crystal-clear fount of all reliable
knowledge and coherence, as it has for so long been presumed to be.
Its method is not that of <u>detachment</u> but rather of <u>involvement</u>. It
rests, no less than our other ways of achieving meaning, upon
various commitments which we personally share" (M. Polanyi and

H. Prosch, *Meaning*, Univ. of Chicago Press, 1975, p. 63; emphasis in original). Postempiricist philosophers of science (e.g., Polanyi, Thomas Kuhn, Norwood Hanson, Paul Feyerabend, and others) incorporate this insight into their arguments about the rationality of science (see, for example, H. Brown, *Perception, Theory, and Commitment: The New Philosophy of Science*, Univ. of Chicago Press, 1977). Thus, it seems reasonable to say that tacit or personal knowing plays an important role in <u>all</u> forms of scientific investigation. **See also PROPOSITIONAL KNOWLEDGE, *WELTANSCHAUUNG*.**

TEXT   There are at least three related ways in which to think of the importance of the notion of 'text' in qualitative work. The broadest conception is explained by Clifford Geertz in his 1980 essay "Blurred Genres: The Refiguration of Social Thought" (reprinted in C. Geertz, *Local Knowledge*, Basic Books, 1983). We can ask, "What analogies do social scientists use to imagine what social life (the object of social inquiry) is like and how it can be best explained?" Traditionally, social science has looked to analogies drawn from the natural sciences to explain social life in terms of laws, forces, structures, and mechanisms. In the past two decades or so it has, however, become increasingly popular for social theorists to borrow analogies from the humanities. That is, to think of viewing and explaining *social action* as being like moves by players in a game, performances by actors in a drama, and sentences in a text. Of these three kinds of analogies, the textual analogy is, as Geertz suggests, perhaps the most venturesome and least obvious. Yet, Geertz notes that it is a potentially very powerful analogy, not least because it refigures social explanation: "To see social institutions, social customs, social changes as in some sense 'readable' is to alter our whole sense of what [sociological] interpretation is and shift it toward modes of thought more familiar to the translator, the exegete, or the iconographer than to the test giver, the factor analyst, or the pollster" (p. 31).

The second, more narrow or technical understanding of 'text' is specifically related to the textual paradigm of *hermeneutics*. The phenomenon of the text—biblical, classical, legal, and so on—and the interrelated issues of interpretation, language, and meaning in understanding a text lies at the heart of what it means to do hermeneutics. Although the work of Martin Heidegger (1889-1976) and

Hans-Georg Gadamer established the notion of ontological hermeneutics—not simply a textual hermeneutics but a universal *philosophical hermeneutics* that reveals that interpretation is an indelible
feature of human experience—the 'text' still serves as the paradigm
for philosophical hermeneutics. To be considered a viable framework for the social sciences, philosophical hermeneutics had to be
extended to address the subject matter of the social sciences. This
required an argument by analogy: Social action can be read like
a written text. This argument is most clearly explained by Paul
Ricoeur (see "The Model of the Text: Meaningful Action Considered
as a Text," in Paul Ricoeur, *Hermeneutics and the Human Sciences*, ed.
and trans. J. B. Thompson, Cambridge Univ. Press, 1981). Ricoeur
accepted the premise that the object of social science was meaningful
social action construed as a whole and he proceeded to explain why
(1) this object displayed some of the same features constitutive of a
written text, and (2) the methodology of hermeneutics employs procedures in understanding this object that are similar to those used in
interpreting written texts. Charles Taylor ("Interpretation and the
Sciences of Man," *Review of Metaphysics*, 1971, 25: 3-51) also develops
this analogy in his defense of hermeneutical social science. Ricoeur's
and Taylor's arguments lend support to the broad textual analogy
for social theorizing explained by Geertz.

A third understanding of 'text' is offered by some poststructuralists who, following Jacques Derrida, hold that everything (life
experiences, events, relationships, activities, practices, cultural artifacts, and so on) is a text. This radical extension of the textual
paradigm is often referred to as pantextualism, textualism, or the
primacy of language. In this view, texts have several characteristics:
(1) They are 'writerly' texts capable of, indeed requiring, rewriting
in every encounter by a reader (vs. a traditional notion of 'readerly'
texts destined for a passive reader and read for a specific message);
(2) Every text is related to every other text; this is known as intertextuality; (3) Every text is open ended and indeterminate and thus the
site of an infinite number of interpretations. For an application of
this idea to sociological inquiry, see N. Denzin, *Symbolic Interactionism and Cultural Studies*, Blackwell, 1992. **See also HUMAN ACTION,
POSTSTRUCTURALISM.**

TEXTUALIZATION See TRANSCRIPTION.

THEORETICAL CANDOR This is a procedure for establishing *validity* of analysis and interpretation in ethnography suggested by Roger Sanjek ("On Ethnographic Validity," in *Fieldnotes*, Cornell Univ. Press, 1990). Sanjek explains that disciplinary perspectives and formal theories held by the *fieldworker* determine the site, problems, and objectives brought to the *field*, thereby giving ethnography a particular purpose and meaning. In addition, the fieldworker develops "terrain-specific theories" about people, places, and events that determine much of what is heard and seen. Sanjek argues that fieldworkers must make both kinds of theoretical decisions explicit in their writing. Similar procedures for documenting both the a priori function of theory—its role in shaping hypotheses, problems, and propositions to be examined as well as the events, objects, interactions, and people the fieldworker looks for in the field—and the use of theory in developing local accounts of significance as the fieldwork unfolds—are emphasized by many methodologists in qualitative inquiry.

THEORETICAL SAMPLING See GROUNDED THEORY METHODOLOGY.

THEORETICAL SATURATION See GROUNDED THEORY METHODOLOGY.

THEORY Discussion about the nature and role of theory in qualitative work is focused on four issues: (1) theory as the aim of the social sciences; (2) the relationship between theory and observation; (3) the role of theory in qualitative work; and (4) types of theory.

  Theory as the aim of the social sciences: Theory is generally understood to refer to a unified, systematic *explanation* of a diverse range of social phenomena. Examples from different social science disciplines include exchange theory, kinship theory, cognitive dissonance theory, and Keynesian economic theory. Although what constitutes an adequate account of explanatory social theory is a matter of some debate, there is general agreement among naturalists, some critical social scientists, and pluralists that developing explanatory social theory is the proper goal of the social sciences (see, for example, R. J. Bernstein, *The Restructuring of Social and Political Theory*, Univ. of Pennsylvania Press, 1976). Theory is here defined as empirical and explanatory and is distinguished from the accumulation of empirical generalizations in social science. Ideally, social theory will take a form approximating the form it takes in the physical sciences, that is, a tightly interrelated set of propositions that includes basic invariants or laws that allow for grand or formal theorizing. Using this definition of what it means to do social science as a criterion for what counts as "science," a naturalist would argue that inquirers who simply develop concepts, inquirers who gather up observations and make empirical generalizations, or inquirers who simply describe phenomena are not really achieving the aim of social scientific inquiry. All of those kinds of things may be necessary, but they are not sufficient for realizing the aim of the social sciences.

This understanding of theory is important for several reasons. First, this conception of causal, explanatory social theory (also spoken of as the aim *Erklärung*) is strongly criticized by antinaturalists or defenders of phenomenological and hermeneutic approaches to the social sciences. Second, efforts to defend explanatory theory as the proper goal of social inquiry account for some of the quarrels over the nature of social scientific investigation <u>within</u> interpretive work. In educational ethnography, for example, the British ethnographer Martyn Hammersley has chastised the field for being too descriptive and not attentive to this goal of developing and testing theory. In anthropology in the 1960s and 1970s the common view was that rigorous, scientific, nomothetic study was superior to idiographic, culture-specific study—that is, ethnography. Since the late 1970s the sentiment in anthropology has turned in the opposite direction: Culture-specific ethnographic study of meaning, symbols, and language is regarded as more important than causal, explanatory theorizing. Third, many poststructuralists totally reject efforts to develop explanatory theory of any kind (see *explanation*).

<u>Relationship between theory and observation.</u> The philosophies of *logical positivism* and *logical empiricism* assigned epistemological priority to observation statements. In other words, knowledge was said to rest on unambiguous observations. Concepts and theories were entirely dependent for their meaning on the particular observation statements into which they could be unpacked. Thus, the logical empiricist Herbert Feigl (See "The 'Orthodox' View of Theories," in M. Radner and S. Winokur, eds., *Minnesota Studies in the*

T

Philosophy of Science IV, Univ. of Minnesota Press, 1970) argued that theoretical concepts grow out of the "soil" of observation: Theory is meaningful <u>precisely because</u> of "an 'upward seepage' of meaning from the observation terms to the theoretical concepts." These philosophies drew a sharp distinction between theory (concepts) and observation. They regarded fact or empirical evidence as more important than theoretical concerns in the construction, judgment, and accumulation of scientific knowledge claims. They denied that theoretical or more general metaphysical commitments played any significant role in the development of scientific knowledge. The following famous statement from David Hume's (1711-1776) *Enquiry Concerning Human Understanding* served as a motto of sorts for the hard-line positivists of the Vienna Circle who argued that only analytic and synthetic statements had any purchase in forming testable knowledge claims: "When we run over libraries, persuaded of these principles, what havoc must we make? If we take in our hand any volume of divinity or school metaphysics, for instance, let us ask: Does it contain any abstract reasoning concerning quantity or number? No. Does it contain any experimental reasoning concerning matter of fact and existence? No. Commit it then to the flames, for it can contain nothing but sophistry and illusion" (quoted in A. J. Ayer, *Logical Positivism,* Free Press, 1959, p. 10).

This sharp theory-observation separation was strongly criticized by a number of philosophers including Thomas Kuhn, Michael Polanyi, Paul Feyerabend, Imre Lakatos, and others. They argued that considerations such as *tacit knowledge,* prior theory, metaphysical commitments, and the like influenced the making of observations, decisions about what constituted fact, and so forth. They challenged the relative priority of observation statements over theoretical statements and attempted to restore theoretical considerations to an equal footing with observation statements in our picture of the development of scientific knowledge.

The various philosophies of science that came after logical positivism (*postpositivism*) are concerned with defining and explicating the role that theoretical commitments, conceptual schemes, beliefs, assumptions, and the like play in the conduct of scientific inquiry and the construction of scientific claims. There is now general agreement that the formation, testing, and success of scientific theories is not solely an empirical matter, that is, it does not depend on some kind of unshakable foundation of observations. Rather, there is some sort of dynamic interplay between theory and observations. Thus, postpositivism, in general, is concerned with 'rehabilitating the theoretical' by examining how interpretive theoretical commitments (i.e., behaviorism, symbolic interactionism, materialism, critical theory, feminist theory, structuralism, poststructuralism, and so forth) and values shape, organize, and give meaning to our observations about people and society.

As a consequence of abandoning a strict observation-theory distinction, it is now generally recognized that atheoretical investigation is impossible. A simplistic Baconian view (something like, first gather the facts through what we see, hear, touch, and so on, and then form knowledge claims by induction) simply does not adequately describe the activity of scientific inquiry. We know that inquiry does not start with pure observation because some kind of theory precedes the collection of observations. We also know that observations do not provide an unshakable foundation for theory because all observations are fallible. James Garrison (see "The Impossibility of Atheoretical Science," *Journal of Educational Thought*, 1988, 22: 21-26) uses the Meno paradox to illustrate the point here: The paradox says that all inquiry is impossible because either we know what we seek, in which case why search for it, or we have no idea what we seek, in which case how would we recognize it? The way out of this paradox is to recognize that we have partial foreknowledge of the phenomena we inquire into. Prior conceptual structure (theory and method) provides the foreknowledge necessary to initiate and guide the observations we make as inquirers. Garrison further argues that those who claim to do atheoretical inquiry actually do one or more of the following: (1) They hold their theories tacitly, in which case they need to reflect on them and state them explicitly; (2) they hold them explicitly but deliberately withhold them from public view; (3) they pack structural concepts that properly belong to theory into their methodology, where they are hidden from their view as well as ours.

Two misunderstandings arise in the discourse on qualitative inquiry when this generally accepted idea about the impossibility of atheoretical research is ignored. The first is a <u>naive</u> *ethnographic naturalism.* Ethnographic naturalism is based on the presupposition of being 'faithful' to the phenomenon under investigation: The social world must be understood as it is in its 'natural' state by not imposing some prior commitment to scientific method. This doctrine is a much-welcomed antidote to the positivistic emphasis on the centrality of method (fidelity or 'faithfulness' to methodological principles); however, it can be wrongly taken to mean something very much like observation and description of the way things 'really are,' free of any prior conceptual scheme or theory. A little reflection reveals why this is not possible: The doctrine of ethnographic naturalism (as manifest in symbolic interactionism, phenomenology, ethnomethodology, naturalistic inquiry, and the like) is itself a cognitive theoretical frame that orients the inquiry. Furthermore, it is impossible to observe and describe what goes on in 'natural' settings without some theory of what is relevant to observe, how what is observed is to be named, and so on. This is readily evident when we compare, say, the efforts of materialists and idealists to understand and portray the same culture. Even seemingly simple or mundane typological schemes for organizing and classifying data are theoretically informed.

A second similar misunderstanding surrounds the practice of grounded theory. Again, the fallacy seems to be that the inquirer enters the inquiry tabula rasa and collects data, and then theory actually emerges inductively from the data. In fact, grounded theory is a complex process of both induction and deduction, guided by prior theoretical commitments and conceptual schemes. In this means of analysis, as well as in any other attempt to move from fieldnotes to concepts and interpretations, the task is far from purely inductive and inferential. To be sure, the grounded theory approach emphasizes fidelity to the phenomenon under study by arguing against grand or speculative theories. Grounded theory is not, however, simply a methodological scheme for initiating and guiding inquiry. It requires prior theoretical understandings as well; something very much like what the literary theorist Northrop Frye called an "educated imagination." Consider, for example, the emphasis on the importance of a 'coding paradigm' in grounded theory (see A. L. Strauss, *Qualitative Analysis for Social Scientists*, Cambridge Univ. Press, 1987). This paradigm helps the inquirer to go beyond simple naming (itself requiring a theory) to construct conceptually dense codes that identify the conditions, interactions among actors, strategies and tactics, and consequences associated with what is named. To engage in such coding activity the inquirer must have 'theoretical sensitivity' that facilitates the identification and interrelation of these conditions. Or consider the central notion of theoretical sampling in grounded theory: One decides what to sample on the basis of its contribution to the evolving analytical scheme. This scheme arises from prior knowledge of potentially relevant concepts, ideas, and other schemes continually tested for adequacy against the data at hand.

   The role of theory in qualitative inquiry. Theory plays a role both in orienting the fieldworker to the object of study and in writing about what one has researched. A moment's reflection on, for example, the existentialist posture of fieldworkers like Peter and Patricia Adler or Jack Douglas, the commitment of Paul Rabinow to phenomenology, or Shirley Brice Heath's sociolinguistic conceptual scheme reveals that one enters the field with a theoretical language and attitude. That substantive theory is essential for making meaning out of or interpreting the data needs little further explanation. There are, of course, disagreements on whether theory is best employed and emphasized in *fieldwork* or *deskwork*. John VanMaanen (*Tales of the Field*, Univ. of Chicago Press, 1988), for example, notes that confessionalist ethnographers, unlike, say, realist ethnographers, seem to find theory most relevant during the writing or deskwork phase: "Theory doesn't determine the fieldwork experience, but it may provide the dictionary with which it is read" (pp. 97-98).

   Types of theory. Although the formal definition limits the term "theory" to systematic, causal explanatory accounts of phenomena, it is commonplace to talk of theory in a less formal way. Thus, theory may be said to come in all sizes. One way of classifying various understandings of theory is in terms of levels of sophistication, organization, and comprehensiveness. At the simplest level there are theoretical ideas or just concepts. Ethnographers, for example, operate with the concept of *culture* foremost in mind, although very few actually are committed to or develop a very detailed theory of culture. Concepts point the inquirer in a general direction but do not give a very specific set of instructions for what to see. Working at the level of concepts is not flashy, as Harry Wolcott (*Transforming Quali-tative Data*, Sage, 1994) points out; and it is hard to squeeze theory out of a concept. But then, by dealing only with the meaning of concepts, the inquirer avoids a lot of the academic posturing so common in exchanges over theory. Wolcott advises that working with concepts may be especially appealing for fieldworkers who are interested in searching out interpretations for data rather than seek-ing illustrations for theory (see *analytic generalization*). On the downside, he notes that those fieldworkers satisfied with using concepts to orient their research must often deal with accusations that they lack precision, like hunters using a shotgun rather than a rifle, or shoppers who are just looking.

A step or so up the ladder of sophistication are theoretical frameworks. These are formal theories to distinguish them from informal or simply personal conceptual schemes. They are interre-lated sets of propositions, concepts, and assumptions that constitute comprehensive perspectives or models. Sometimes called 'theoreti-cal paradigms,' these frameworks are both embedded in and par-tially constitute research traditions in the social sciences. Included here are the major theoretical models of anthropology, sociology, and psychology (e.g., structural functionalism, symbolic interactionism, conflict theory, behaviorism, critical theory, and so on). Within the broad designation of formal theory are the categories of substantive, middle-range, and grand theories. The best way to distinguish among these types of formal theory is to think in terms of the scope of their application. Substantive theories hover low over the data, as Clifford Geertz says; they explain the case at hand—some phenome-non in restricted, concrete populations, times, and settings. Middle-range theories are somewhat more general or abstract. They explain a phenomenon in a wider variety of settings and are typically developed from multiple comparisons. Grand theory (e.g., social Darwinism, Marxism, Parsons's social systems theory, Nicholas Luhmann's social systems theory) explains large, complex catego-ries of phenomena. In the mid-1950s and 1960s several sociologists offered strong criticisms of grand, abstract theory (e.g., C. Wright Mills's *The Sociological Imagination*, Oxford Univ. Press, 1959; Barney Glaser and Anslem Strauss, *The Discovery of Grounded Theory*, Aldine, 1967). As an alternative, they often argued for theory that was built more from the bottom up and took more careful account of actual cases. **See also** EXPLANATION, THEORETICAL CANDOR.

THEORY-OBSERVATION DISTINCTION   See THEORY.

THEORY-PRACTICE RELATIONSHIP   See PRAXIS.

THICK DESCRIPTION   Careful, detailed description of *social action* is said to be the foundation of ethnography and qualitative inquiry more generally. The primacy of description goes hand in glove with the belief in *ethnographic naturalism* and with the phenomenological orientation of much qualitative work. Description is thought to be fundamental to understanding or interpreting social action, but not just any kind of description will do. Following advice given by Clifford Geertz in his widely cited 1983 essay "Thick Description: Toward an Interpretive Theory of Culture," many qualitative inquirers emphasize the importance of 'thick' as opposed to 'thin' description. Yet, it is not entirely clear just what thick description is. Most efforts to define it emphasize that thick description is not simply a matter of amassing relevant detail. Rather, to thickly describe social action is actually to begin to interpret it by recording the circumstances, meanings, intentions, strategies, motivations, and so on that characterize a particular episode. It is this interpretive characteristic of description rather than detail per se that makes it thick.

Description is often said to form the empirical basis for interpretation. James Clifford ("Notes on (Field)notes" in R. Sanjek, ed., *Fieldnotes*, Cornell Univ. Press, 1990, p. 67) notes that ethnographers often think of description as providing "a body of knowledge prefigured for theoretical development." Harry Wolcott (*Transforming Qualitative Data*, Sage, 1994, p. 55) echoes a similar view in arguing that a descriptive account is foundational for the work of analysis and interpretation; it is "at the heart of qualitative inquiry." But what does it mean to say that descriptive data are an empirical base? Only the most naive fieldworker would claim that there is such a thing as pure description or 'raw' data. The knowledge that all observation is theory laden is generally accepted. Simply carving up the field of social action by deciding what to observe and what not to observe requires some foreknowledge of what is important to attend to. And it is generally recognized that descriptions will be mediated by

T

disciplinary biases, choice of language, personal experiences, and the like. But many postmodern ethnographers offer a more radical critique of the role of description in ethnographic work that has its origins in these widely accepted ideas. They hold that the very idea of description as forming the empirical ground for qualitative work suggests, in Stephen Tyler's words (see "Postmodern Ethnography: From Document of the Occult to Occult Document," in J. Clifford and G. E. Marcus, eds., *Writing Culture*, Univ. of California Press, 1986, p. 131), a "visualist rhetoric of representation" or what Clifford calls an unmediated "specular, representational relation to culture" (p. 68). Tyler argues that postmodern ethnographies are nonrepresentational; they "evoke" rather than "represent." Postmodern ethnographic experiments are efforts aimed at decentering fieldworker-controlled and authored description as the basis for accounts of meaningful social action. Decentering is achieved by experimenting with other kinds of bases for accounts of action (e.g., transcriptions), using dialogue and novelistic genres, and so on. See also INSCRIPTION, REPRESENTATION, TRANSCRIPTION.

TRANSCRIPTION   This is a written account—a text—of what a *respondent* or informant said in response to a fieldworker's query or what respondents said to one another in conversation. The point is to record and prepare a record of the respondent's own words. The transcription may result from retyped handwritten notes or audio recordings. When a fieldworker records a speech made by a respondent, a respondent's description of an event, a conversation between respondents, a series of answers to a set of interview questions, and so on, the fieldworker is preparing a transcription. James Clifford ("On Ethnographic Authority," *Representations*, 1983, 1(2): 146-188) has argued that when reports of *fieldwork* are based largely on texts produced through transcription they may have the effect of breaking up the monological authority of the fieldworker-as-privileged-author or interpreter of human action. Yet, he and other ethnographers caution that transcription is not some kind of innocent recording of the way things really are. John VanMaanen (*Tales of the Field,* Univ. of Chicago Press, 1988, p. 95) states that transcriptions (as well as all other forms of *fieldnotes*) are mediated "many times over—by the fieldworker's own standards of relevance for what is of interest;

by the historically situated queries put to informants; by the norms current in the fieldworker's professional community for what is proper work; by the self-reflection demanded of both the fieldworker and the informant; by the intentional and unintentional ways a fieldworker or informant is misled; and by the fieldworker's mere presence on the scene as an observer and participant." VanMaanen borrows from Paul Ricoeur the term "textualization"—the process whereby 'unwritten' behavior, beliefs, traditions, and so on become fixed, discrete, particular kinds of data—to claim that it is only in textualized form that data yield to analysis. Hence, he concludes "the process of analysis is not dependent on the events themselves [as recorded in allegedly innocent transcriptions], but on a second-order, textualized, fieldworker-dependent version of events." **See also** INSCRIPTION, INTERVIEWING, TEXT, THICK DESCRIPTION.

TRANSFERABILITY   See GENERALIZATION, TRUSTWORTHINESS CRITERIA.

TRIANGULATION   This is a procedure used to establish the fact that the criterion of *validity* has been met. The fieldworker makes inferences from data, claiming that a particular set of data supports a particular definition, theme, assertion, hypothesis, claim, etc. Triangulation is a means of checking the integrity of the inferences one draws. It can involve the use of multiple data sources, multiple investigators, multiple theoretical perspectives, multiple methods, or all of these (see N. K. Denzin, *The Research Act*, 3rd ed., Prentice Hall, 1989). The central point of the procedure is to examine a single social phenomenon from more than one vantage point. For example, to understand the nature of communication between geriatric patients and internists in an outpatient clinic, the fieldworker might compare data from early and late phases of fieldwork, from different patient-physician pairs, from different times in the temporal cycle of the encounter (taking the medical history—testing—diagnosis—prescribing a treatment plan—follow-up), and so forth. Or data from observations of patient-physician interactions may be compared with data from interviews with each party, and so on. The often unwarranted assumption about use of triangulation is that data from different sources or methods must necessarily converge on or be aggregated to reveal the truth. Martyn Hammersley and Paul

T

Atkinson (*Ethnography: Principles in Practice,* Tavistock, 1983, pp. 199-200) advise: "One should not . . . adopt a naively 'optimistic' view that the aggregation of data from different sources will un-problematically add up to produce a more complete picture . . . differences between sets or types of data may be just as important and illuminating. . . . What is involved in triangulation is not just a matter of checking whether inferences are valid, but of discovering which inferences are valid."

TRUSTWORTHINESS CRITERIA   One set of *criteria* that have been offered for judging the quality or goodness of qualitative inquiry. In *Naturalistic Inquiry* (Sage, 1985), Yvonna Lincoln and Egon Guba sought to establish criteria (and associated procedures) that were more appropriate than traditional epistemic criteria (e.g., internal and external validity) and procedures for judging the trustworthiness of naturalistic investigations. Trustworthiness was defined as that quality of an investigation (and its findings) that made it noteworthy to audiences. The authors developed four criteria that served as the naturalist's equivalents for conventional criteria: (1) Credibility (parallel to internal validity) addressed the issue of the inquirer providing assurances of the fit between respondents' views of their life ways and the inquirer's reconstruction and representation of same. (2) Transferability (parallel to external validity) dealt with the issue of *generalization* in terms of case-to-case transfer. It concerned the inquirer's responsibility for providing readers with sufficient information on the case studied (Case A) such that readers could establish the degree of similarity between the case studied and the case to which findings might be transferred (Case B). (3) Dependability (parallel to reliability) focused on the process of the inquiry and the inquirer's responsibility for ensuring that the process was logical, traceable, and documented. (4) Confirmability (parallel to objectivity) was concerned with establishing the fact that the data and interpretations of an inquiry were not merely figments of the inquirer's imagination. It called for linking assertions, findings, interpretations, and so on to the data themselves in readily discernible ways. For each of these criteria, Lincoln and Guba also specified a set of procedures useful in meeting the criteria. For example, *auditing* was described as a procedure useful for establishing both dependability and confirmability; *member check* and *peer debriefing*, among other procedures, were defined as most appropriate for credibility; and so on. Several years later, in *Fourth Generation Evaluation* (Sage, 1989), Guba and Lincoln reevaluated this initial set of criteria. They explained that trustworthiness criteria were parallel, quasi-foundational, and clearly intended to be analogs to conventional criteria. Furthermore, they held that trustworthiness criteria were principally methodological criteria and thereby largely ignored aspects of the quality of the inquiry concerned with outcome, product, and negotiation. Hence, they advanced a second set of criteria called *authenticity criteria* arguing that this second set was better aligned with the constructivist epistemology that informed their definition of qualitative inquiry. **See also PROBLEM OF CRITERIA, VALIDITY.**

T

UNDERSTANDING The English equivalent of the German term *Verstehen*. Understanding the meaning of *social action* is often spoken of as the goal of the human sciences (versus *explanation* as the goal of the natural sciences). **See also** VERSTEHEN.

USE OF QUALITATIVE INQUIRY See GENERALIZATION.

VALIDATION HERMENEUTICS Also called conservative *herme-neutics* or objectivist hermeneutics, this approach defines herme-neutics as a method for the validation of the meaning embedded in a text. Its principal advocates are the legal historian Emilio Betti (see the excerpt of the original German work in "Hermeneutics as the General Methodology of the *Geisteswissenschaften*" in J. Bleicher, ed., *Contemporary Hermeneutics*, Routledge and Kegan Paul, 1980) and the American professor of literature E. D. Hirsch (*Validity in Interpretation*, Yale Univ. Press, 1967; *The Aims of Interpretation*, Univ. of Chicago Press, 1976). Both Betti and Hirsch argue that an author's intended meaning of a text is a fixed, determinate entity or object that can be depicted or portrayed accurately. This meaning is the external reference point against which competing interpretations of a text are judged to be valid or invalid. This definition of hermeneutics contrasts sharply with both *philosophical hermeneutics* and *deconstructionism.*

VALIDITY   In ordinary usage, validity is a property of a statement, argument, or procedure. To call one of those things "valid" is to indicate that it is sound, cogent, well grounded, justifiable, or logically correct. Psychologically, validity means having confidence in one's statements or knowledge claims. In social science, validity is one of the *criteria* that traditionally serve as a benchmark for inquiry. Validity is an epistemic criterion: To say that the findings of social scientific investigations are (or must be) valid is to argue that the findings are in fact (or must be) true and certain. "True" here means that the findings accurately represent the phenomena to which they refer and "certain" means that the findings are backed by evidence—or warranted—and there are no good grounds for doubting the findings or the evidence for the findings in question is stronger than the evidence for alternative findings.

There is much discomfort with and some outright rejection of this criterion among some social inquirers committed to constructivist, postmodernist, feminist, and pragmatic perspectives. Their objections are many and interrelated. A few of the more salient ones are singled out here. First, they reject naive or direct *realism*—the idea that we can have direct, unmediated knowledge of the world. They argue that if truth means our ideas about the world must correspond to the way the world really is and if validity is a test of this correspondence, then there can be no validity because there is no unmediated, observer-independent account of experience that an account can mirror or correspond to. Second, and in a related way, critics reject the notion that we 'discover' the truth about the world, that is, that truth is somehow 'out there.' They hold that all accounts of the world are language bound. Thus, if there is such a thing as truth it is arbitrary, and validity would be relative to some particular language system or worldview. Third, critics reject the association of validity with *objectivism*—the doctrine that there must be permanent, ahistorical benchmarks or foundations for judging the truth of claims. Any attempt to associate validity with objectivism is greeted at least with *skepticism.* One additional, even stronger objection to truth and validity comes from radical postmodernists who hold that the very idea of truth as essential to knowledge or as a goal of science is a modernist, Enlightenment value associated with order, rules, logic, rationality, and reason, all of which are considered suspect at best and, at worst, oppressive.

What this all means is that there are several different stances on the meaning of validity in qualitative work. At least four different positions can be identified: (1) Fallibilistic validity: Here, validity is understood as a test of whether an account accurately represents the social phenomena to which it refers. Yet, no claim is made that an account actually 'reproduces' an independently existing reality or that a valid account is absolutely certain. Defenders of this view hold that one can have good reasons for accepting an account as true or false, yet an account is always fallible. Martyn Hammersley (*Reading Ethnographic Research*, Longman, 1990), for example, argues that we judge the validity of an account by checking whether it is plausible; whether it is credible given the nature of the phenomenon being investigated, the circumstances of the research, and the characteristics of the researcher; and, if we doubt either plausibility or credibility, by inspecting the credibility of evidence offered in support of the claim. On this view, all procedures typically cited as means of establishing validity (e.g., *analytic induction* for testing hypotheses, *triangulation, member check,* providing fieldwork evidence, *theoretical candor,* and so on) are nothing more or less than fallible means of making a case for a plausible and credible account. (2) Relativized validity: Here, the validity of an account is relative to the standards of a particular community at a particular place and time. The validity of an account or interpretation is judged in terms of the consensus about words, concepts, standards, and so on in a given community of interpreters (see, for example, Stanley Fish, *Is There a Text in This Class?* Harvard Univ. Press, 1980; Gareth Morgan, ed., *Beyond Method,* Sage, 1983). (3) No validity: The most radical of postmodernists would argue that it is meaningless to talk of a 'true' account of the world; there are only different linguistically mediated social constructions. On this radical perspectivalist view, validity is an empty issue because no single interpretation or account can be judged superior to any other. There is only the endless interplay of different interpretations (see, for example, Jacques Derrida, *Spurs: Nietzsche's Styles,* Univ. of Chicago Press, 1979). (4) Nonepistemic validity: Here validity is made into something other than an epistemic criterion. Validity may be interpreted as a criterion of good communication or dialogue; the focus shifts from whether an account is true to how the account was formed in conversation between inquirer and participants. Validity may also be interpreted as a criterion of action such that an account is considered valid if it leads to change, empowerment, and so on. For different ways in which validity is defined as a nonepistemic criterion, see the discussion of *authenticity criteria* in Egon Guba and Yvonna Lincoln, *Fourth Generation Evaluation*, Sage, 1989; Steinar Kvale, "The Social Construction of Validity," *Qualitative Inquiry*, 1995, 1(1): 19-40; Patti Lather, "Fertile Obsession: Validity After Poststructuralism," *Sociological Quarterly*, 1993, 34(4): 673-693. **See also PROBLEM OF CRITERIA.**

VALUE-FREE SOCIAL SCIENCE See DISINTERESTED SOCIAL SCIENCE/ SCIENTIST.

VERISIMILITUDE   The term originates in Karl Popper's (1902-1994) philosophy of science. Popper held that the goal of science is increasing verisimilitude; where verisimilitude meant an approximation toward or closeness to the truth about the way the world really is. He argued that we could compare scientific theories by looking at the relative amounts of truth or falsity contained within each theory. This proved to be an indefensible position, although the notion of verisimilitude has been salvaged in modified form by the philosopher of science W. H. Newton-Smith in *The Rationality of Science* (Routledge and Kegan Paul, 1968).

The term "verisimilitude," as it appears in discussions about the methodologies of qualitative inquiry, is used in ways quite different from that intended by Popper. Three overlapping definitions of the term, all dealing with a quality of the text, include: (1) Verisimilitude as a criterion (others include plausibility, internal coherence, and correspondence to readers' own experience) sometimes cited as important for judging narrative inquiry. A narrative account (referring either to the narratives generated from or by respondents or to the narrative report produced by the inquirer) is said to exhibit the quality of verisimilitude when it has the appearance of truth or reality. (Note: What Popper meant by approximation to the truth is quite different from appearance of truth.) (2) Verisimilitude as a

V

criterion for judging the evocative power or sense of authenticity of a textual portrayal: A style of writing that draws readers into the experiences of respondents in such a way that those experiences can be felt. (3) Verisimilitude as the relationship of a particular text to some agreed on opinions or standards of a particular interpretive community. A particular text (e.g., book review, scholarly essay, speech to a scholarly society, research report, and so on) has verisimilitude to the extent that it conforms to the conventions of its genre. A related word in poetics is <u>vraisemblance,</u> which refers broadly to the plausibility of any text and encompasses the three senses of verisimilitude noted above (see J. Culler, *Structuralist Poetics: Structuralism, Linguistics, and the Study of Literature*, Cornell Univ. Press, 1975).

VERSTEHEN   This is a German term for "understanding," used to refer both to the aim of human sciences and to their method. Reacting to the growing prominence of empiricist and positivist epistemologies in the late nineteenth and early twentieth century, the German philosopher and historian Wilhelm Dilthey (1833-1911) set out to establish the unique nature of historical and cultural knowledge. He argued that what fundamentally distinguished the natural sciences (*Naturwissenschaften*) from the human (mental) sciences (*Geisteswissenschaften*) was that the former aimed at developing causal explanations (*Erklärung*) from the outside, so to speak, through the use of general laws, whereas the latter aimed at understanding meaning from the agent or actor's point of view (*Verstehen*) by grasping the subjective consciousness of action from the inside: "Nature we explain; psychic life we understand." Dilthey relied heavily on the analysis of inner, psychic experience as distinct from (but related to) outer experience of external nature. He emphasized that the social inquirer must engage in a psychological reenactment (*Nacherleben*) or imaginative reconstruction of the experience of human actors to understand human social life and history. Hence, his view of *Verstehen* had strong overtones of psychologism (the doctrine that reduces the objects of consciousness to mental states). This distinction between the natural and human sciences was further elaborated by neo-Kantian philosophers Wilhelm Windelband (1848-1915) and Heinrich Rickert (1863-1936), who objected to the psychologism

V

inherent in Dilthey's view. Windelband argued that the natural sciences seek nomothetic knowledge (general laws) while the historical sciences seek to describe unique events (idiographic knowledge). Unlike Dilthey, he held that there was no essential difference in the <u>objects</u> that the two sciences studied, only a difference in <u>method.</u> Any kind of object (e.g., mental events, physical objects) could be studied by means of both methods. Windelband claimed that positivism's error was in believing that every event must be viewed nomothetically. Rickert developed a connection between ideal or transcendent cultural values and historical events, arguing that it was only through grasping this connection that the meaning of historical events could be made clear. He used the term *Kulturwissenschaften*—cultural sciences—to signal a revision of Dilthey's focus on inner, psychic experience.

Max Weber's (1864-1920) efforts to establish an interpretive sociology (*Verstehende* Sociology) predicated on an understanding of actors' perspectives of their social action was, in turn, indebted to the work of these predecessors. Weber ("Basic Sociological Terms" in *Economy and Society,* G. Roth and C. Wittich, eds., Bedminster, 1968) distinguished two kinds of *Verstehen:* "direct observational understanding" in which the purpose or meaning of **human action** is immediately apparent, and "explanatory understanding," which required grasping the motivation for human behavior by placing the action in some intelligible, inclusive context of meaning. Weber argued that human action is both open to and requires interpretation in terms of the subjective meaning that actors attach to that action. Social scientific (causal) explanation of human action had to be predicated on this kind of understanding.

The phenomenological sociologist Alfred Schutz (1899-1956) sought to clear up the meaning of *Verstehen* by distinguishing three senses of the term (*Collected Papers, Vol. 1,* ed. and trans. M. Natanson, Martinus Nijhoff, 1967): (1) As "the experiential form of common-sense knowledge of human affairs": *Verstehen,* in this definition, has nothing to do with introspection or the subjective states of human agents. Rather, it refers to the intersubjective character of the **life-world** and the complex processes by which human beings come to recognize their own actions and those of their fellow actors as meaningful. (2) As an epistemological problem: The central issue here is how *Verstehen* (as a kind of knowledge) is possible. Here, Schutz drew on Edmund Husserl's (1859-1938) considerable work on the concept of the life-world (*Lebenswelt*). Husserl had argued that the life-world was ontologically prior; all scientific, logical, and mathematical concepts originate in this life-world. The life-world is the grounds of all understanding. (3) As a method unique to the human sciences: Schutz argued that social reality has a specific meaning and relevance structure for human beings living, acting, and thinking within it. *Verstehen* thus refers to a first-order process by which we all interpret the world. The interpretation of the world sought by the social scientist must begin by grasping this first-order understanding. The social scientist then fashions a second-order interpretation of that world by employing the constructs of the social sciences. *Verstehen* thus also means a second-order process, a special means of entry into the life-world, by which the social inquirer seeks to understand the first-order process.

Despite the efforts of Schutz and others to clarify what is meant by *Verstehen* or interpretive understanding, *logical empiricists* (e.g., Theodore Abel and Otto Neurath) seized on the tendency to equate the act of understanding with grasping subjective mental states. They argued that *Verstehen* defined as psychological empathy or getting inside other people's heads was interesting only as a heuristic device for generating objectively testable hypotheses. This logical empiricist formulation of *Verstehen* has persisted to the present day and continues to be refuted. For example, echoing Schutz, Charles Taylor, in his often-cited essay "Interpretation and the Sciences of Man" (originally appeared in *Review of Metaphysics*, 1971, 25: 3-51), argued that *Verstehen* has nothing to do with inner-organic or psychological states but with understanding intersubjective meanings constitutive of social life. These meanings, in turn, are grasped not via empathy but by means of a hermeneutic process. And in defending interpretive anthropology, Clifford Geertz found it necessary to explain (in " 'From the Native's Point of View': On the Nature of Anthropological Understanding" in *Local Knowledge*, Basic Books, 1983) that ethnographers cannot claim "some unique form of psychological closeness" with their subjects. He argued that interpretive understanding of the meaning of human action is forthcoming more from the act of looking over the shoulders of others: "The trick is not to get yourself into some inner correspondence of spirit with your informants. Preferring, like the rest of us, to call their souls their own, they are not going to be altogether keen about such an effort anyhow. The trick is to figure out what the devil they think they are up to." Hans-Georg Gadamer accepted Dilthey's idea that the operation of *Verstehen* is profoundly different from explaining the events of nature, but he too rejected the view that understanding depends on a psychological reenactment of the experiences of human actors. In *Truth and Method* (2nd rev. ed., Crossroads, 1989), he argued "*Verstehen ist sprachgebunden*" ("Understanding is tied to language"). Language is the medium of intersubjectivity and the concrete expression of traditions that give human actions particular meaning. *Verstehen* is achieved by entering into a conversation or dialogue with those traditions.

Jürgen Habermas's (*Knowledge and Human Interests*, trans. J. J. Shapiro, Beacon, 1971) theory of critical social science accepts the view that the historical-hermeneutic sciences aim at interpretive understanding or *Verstehen* serving the **interest** of clarifying the conditions for communication and intersubjectivity. These social sciences stand in contrast to the empirical-analytic sciences that aim at explanation in the interest of controlling and manipulating the social world. Habermas argues, however, that each kind of science, although not reducible to each other, makes the mistake of claiming it provides the fundamental knowledge of human action. He defends a third, more basic, emancipatory cognitive interest that permits the dialectical synthesis of the other two interests and forms the basis of his understanding of a critical social science. **See also** EXPLANATION, HERMENEUTICS, *VERSTEHENDE* SOCIOLOGY.

VERSTEHENDE SOCIOLOGY   This is a shorthand way of referring to several social theories (e.g., *symbolic interactionism, phenomenological sociology, ethnomethodology,* and so on) that assign a central place to *Verstehen* or understanding. These approaches are also often called *hermeneutic* because they accept the premise that interpretation or understanding is the fundamental way that human beings participate in the world. The hermeneutic tradition, however, that traces its roots to Hans-Georg Gadamer and is developed by the social theorists Charles Taylor, Jürgen Habermas, Anthony Giddens,

Paul Ricoeur, and others is actually critical of *Verstehende* Sociology. Criticisms center on two ideas: First, *Verstehende* Sociology confines itself largely to the study of subjective meanings, the meanings that reside within individual actors. The hermeneutic tradition argues that this approach ignores the more general underlying structures of intersubjective meanings. Second, the defenders of hermeneutical approaches argue that *Verstehende* Sociology retains a subject-object dichotomy and an objectivist conception of *method*. **See also PHILO-SOPHICAL HERMENEUTICS.**

VOICE Two overlapping senses of this term are important in contemporary qualitative inquiry; one stems from the literary turn in the social sciences, the other from feminist philosophy. The growing interest in the literary analysis of social science texts involved importing conceptual tools from literary criticism and narratology (the study of the nature, form, and structure of narrative) into social science discourse. "Voice" is one of those concepts that has become a particularly useful tool. It is the set of textual signs that characterizes the narrator in a text. Identifying signs of first-person narratives or third-person narratives is part of this notion. Voice includes analysis of all aspects of a text that provide information about who the narrator is, who "speaks" (see, for example, G. Genette, *Narrative Discourse: An Essay in Method*, Cornell Univ. Press, 1980). The associations between voice, authority, and the representation of social (and natural) phenomena are a central concern in the literary turn in the social sciences. Experiments with multivoiced, dialogic, and polyphonic texts are, in part, efforts to break up or decenter the monological voice of authority of the lone fieldworker who writes as if he or she is transparently and unproblematically reproducing social reality in an ethnographic account.

The concern with the connection between "who speaks," "who is heard," and what is "voiced" or "given a voice" (see, for example, M. M. Bakhtin, *Speech Genres and Other Late Essays*, trans. V. W. McGee, C. Emerson and M. Holquest, eds., Univ. of Texas Press, 1986) is central to much feminist scholarship. Although this scholarship shares the concern with voice as defined in the literary turn (and, in many ways, feminist work actually leads the criticism of authorial voice here), it also addresses issues in the politics of voice,

V

for example, how women's voices have been silenced by means of various social practices (including methodologies of social inquiry); how critiques of these practices can be used to nurture women's voices and bring them to the fore; how women's voices have been absent from social science (and natural science) investigations; and so on. For some examples of feminist concern with voice, see in anthropology M. di Leonardo, ed., *Gender at the Crossroads of Knowledge: Feminist Anthropology in the Postmodern Era,* Univ. of California Press, 1991; in psychology, M. Fine, *Disruptive Voices,* Univ. of Michigan Press, 1992; in sociology, S. Kreiger, *The Mirror Dance,* Temple Univ. Press, 1983 and *Social Science and the Self,* Rutgers Univ. Press, 1991. **See also CRISIS OF REPRESENTATION, LITERARY TURN, FEMINIST EPISTEMOLOGY.**

V

W

WELTANSCHAUUNG A German term for "worldview" or "philosophy of life." The *'Weltanschauung* analysts' was a name given to
several philosophers of science (including Stephen Toulmin,
Thomas Kuhn, Norwood Hanson, and Paul Feyerabend, among
others) who were highly critical of how logical positivist epistemology construed the rationality of science as completely free of issues
of human judgment. In contrast, they claimed that scientific theorizing was dependent not only on empirical observations but also on
the scientist's worldview or conceptual perspective, which determined which questions are worth investigating and which answers
are acceptable. For a summary of the views of these analysts and
criticism of their ideas, see Chap. 5 in Frederick Suppe, ed., *The
Structure of Scientific Theories*, 2nd ed., Univ. of Illinois Press, 1977.

■ List of Key References and Suggested Readings

The following list includes the primary citations appearing in the entries on the previous pages as well as a few additional references. Virtually all of the references are secondary sources. The list is organized by broad and not necessarily exclusive categories; some references could be placed in more than one category. Only books and book chapters are listed to restrict an already rather long list.

Critical Social Science/Critical Theory

Benhabib, S., *Critique, Norm, and Utopia: A Study of the Foundations of Critical Theory.* New York: Columbia University Press, 1986.

Bronner, S. E., and Kellner, D. M., *Critical Theory and Society: A Reader.* London: Routledge, 1989.

Carr, W., *For Education: Towards a Critical Educational Inquiry.* Oxford: Open University, 1995.

Fay, B., *Critical Social Science.* Ithaca, NY: Cornell University Press, 1987.

Habermas, J., *Knowledge and Human Interests,* trans. J. J. Shapiro. Boston: Beacon, 1971.

Habermas, J., *Theory of Communicative Action, Vol. 1—Reason and Rationalization of Society, Vol. 2—Lifeworld and System: The Critique of Functional Reason*, trans. T. McCarthy. Boston: Beacon, 1981.

Hoy, D. C., and McCarthy, T., *Critical Theory*. Oxford: Basil Blackwell, 1994.

McCarthy, T., *The Critical Theory of Jürgen Habermas*. Cambridge, MA: MIT Press, 1978.

Thomas, J., *Doing Critical Ethnography*. Newbury Park, CA: Sage, 1993.

Ethnography

Atkinson, P., *The Ethnographic Imagination*. London: Routledge, 1992.

Emerson, R. M., ed., *Contemporary Field Research: A Collection of Readings*. Prospect Heights, IL: Waveland, 1988.

Emerson, R. M., Fretz, R. I., and Shaw, L. L., *Writing Ethnographic Fieldnotes*. Chicago: University of Chicago Press, 1995.

Clifford, J., and Marcus, G., eds., *Writing Culture: The Poetics and Politics of Ethnography*. Berkeley: University of California Press, 1986.

Geertz, C., *Local Knowledge*. New York: Basic Books, 1983.

Geertz, C., *The Interpretation of Cultures*. New York: Basic Books, 1973.

Hammersley, M., and Atkinson, P., *Ethnography: Principles in Practice*. London: Tavistock, 1983.

Marcus, G., and Fischer, M., *Anthropology as Cultural Critique*. Chicago: University of Chicago Press, 1986.

Sanjek, R., ed., *Fieldnotes: The Makings of Anthropology*. Ithaca, NY: Cornell University Press, 1990.

VanMaanen, J., *Tales of the Field: On Writing Ethnography*. Chicago: University of Chicago Press, 1988.

Wolcott, H., *Transforming Qualitative Data*. Thousand Oaks, CA: Sage, 1994.

Ethnomethodology, Phenomenological Sociology, *Verstehende* Sociology

Berger, P., and Luckmann, T., *The Social Construction of Reality*. Garden City, NY: Doubleday, 1966.

Garfinkel, H., *Studies in Ethnomethodology*. Englewood Cliffs, NJ: Prentice Hall, 1967.

Giddens, A., *New Rules of Sociological Method*, 2nd rev. ed. Stanford, CA: Stanford University Press, 1993.

Heritage, J., "Ethnomethodology," in A. Giddens and J. Turner, eds., *Social Theory Today*. Stanford, CA: Stanford University Press, 1987.

Schutz, A., *Collected Papers, Vol. 1*, trans. M. Natanson. The Hague, The Netherlands: Martinus Nijhoff, 1967.

Schutz, A., *The Phenomenology of the Social World*. Evanston, IL: Northwestern University Press, 1967.

Outhwaite, W., *Understanding Social Life: The Method Called Verstehen*. Sydney, Australia: Allen and Unwin, 1975.

Weber, M., *The Methodology of the Social Sciences*, trans. and eds., E. A. Shils and H. A. Finch. New York: Free Press, 1949.

Feminist Theory

Alcoff, L., and Potter, E., eds., *Feminist Epistemologies*. London: Routledge, 1993.

Antony, L. M., and Witt, C., eds., *A Mind of One's Own: Feminist Essays on Reason and Objectivity*. Boulder, CO: Westview, 1993.

di Leonarda, M., ed., *Gender at the Crossroads of Knowledge: Feminist Anthropology in the Postmodern Era*. Berkeley: University of California Press, 1991.

Fonow, M. M., and Cook, J. A., eds., *Beyond Methodology: Feminist Scholarship as Lived Research*. Bloomington: Indiana University Press, 1991.

Harding, S., and Hintikka, M. B., eds., *Discovering Reality: Feminist Perspectives on Epistemology, Metaphysics, Methodology, and Philosophy of Science*. Dordrecht, The Netherlands: D. Reidel, 1983.

Nicholson, L. J., ed., *Feminism/Postmodernism*. London: Routledge, 1990.

Reinharz, S., *Feminist Methods in Social Research*. Oxford: Oxford University Press, 1992.

Hermeneutics

Bernstein, R. J., *Beyond Objectivism and Relativism: Science, Hermeneutics, and Praxis*. Philadelphia: University of Pennsylvania Press, 1983.

Bleicher, J., *Contemporary Hermeneutics: Hermeneutics as Method, Philosophy, and Critique*. London: Routledge and Kegan Paul, 1980.

Caputo, J., *Radical Hermeneutics: Repetition, Deconstruction, and the Hermeneutic Project*. Bloomington: Indiana University Press, 1987.

Dunne, J., *Back to the Rough Ground: "Phronesis" and "Techne" in Modern Philosophy and Aristotle*. Notre Dame, IL: University of Notre Dame Press, 1993.

Gadamer, H.-G., *Truth and Method*, 2nd rev. ed. New York: Crossroads, 1990.

Gallagher, S., *Hermeneutics and Education*. Albany: SUNY Press, 1992.

Palmer, R. E., *Hermeneutics: Interpretation in Schleiermacher, Dilthey, Heidegger, and Gadamer*. Evanston, IL: Northwestern University Press, 1969.

Ricoeur, P., *Hermeneutics and the Human Sciences*, ed. and trans. J. B. Thompson. Cambridge: Cambridge University Press, 1981.

Methodology and Methods

Denzin, N. K., *The Research Act*, 3rd ed. Englewood Cliffs, NJ: Prentice Hall, 1989.

Fielding, N. G., and Lee, R. M., *Using Computers in Qualitative Research*. Newbury Park, CA: Sage, 1991.

Guba, E. G., and Lincoln, Y. S., *Naturalistic Inquiry*. Beverly Hills, CA: Sage, 1985.

Lofland, J., and Lofland, L. H., *Analyzing Social Settings*, 3rd ed. Belmont, CA: Wadsworth, 1995.

McCall, G. J., and Simmons, J. L., eds., *Issues in Participant Observation: A Text and a Reader*. Reading, MA: Addison-Wesley, 1969.

Miles, M., and Huberman, A. M., *Qualitative Data Analysis: An Expanded Sourcebook*, 2nd ed. Thousand Oaks, CA: Sage, 1994.

Patton, M. Q., *Qualitative Evaluation and Research Methods*, 2nd ed. Newbury Park, CA: Sage, 1990.

Rubin, H. J., and Rubin, I. S., *Qualitative Interviewing*. Thousand Oaks, CA: Sage, 1995.

Silverman, H., *Interpreting Qualitative Data: Methods for Analyzing Talk, Text, and Interaction*. Newbury Park, CA: Sage, 1993.

Stake, R. E., *The Art of Case Study*. Thousand Oaks, CA: Sage, 1995.

Strauss, A., *Qualitative Analysis for Social Scientists*. Cambridge: Cambridge University Press, 1987.

Strauss, A., and Corbin, J., *Basics of Qualitative Research: Grounded Theory Procedures and Techniques*. Newbury Park, CA: Sage, 1990.

Weitzman, E., and Miles, M. B., *Computer Programs for Qualitative Data Analysis*. Thousand Oaks, CA: Sage, 1994.

Yin, R. C., *Case Study Research*, 2nd ed. Thousand Oaks, CA: Sage, 1994.

Narrative Epistemology and Ontology

Carr, D., *Time, Narrative, and History*. Bloomington: Indiana University Press, 1986.

Polkinghorne, D., *Narrative Knowing and the Human Sciences*. Albany: SUNY Press, 1988.

Ricoeur, P., *Time and Narrative*, 2 vols., trans. K. McLaughlin and D. Pellauer. Chicago: University of Chicago Press, 1984-86.

Participatory Action Research

Freire, P., *Pedagogy of the Oppressed*, trans. M. Bergman Ramos. New York: Herder and Herder, 1970.

Reason, P., ed., *Participation in Human Inquiry*. Thousand Oaks, CA: Sage, 1994.

Whyte, W. F., ed., *Participatory Action Research*. Newbury Park, CA: Sage, 1991.

Philosophy of Social Science

Blaikie, N., *Approaches to Social Enquiry*. Cambridge, MA: Polity Press, 1993.

Chalmers, A. F., *What Is This Thing Called Science?* Queensland, Australia: University of Queensland Press, 1982.

Hollis, M., *The Philosophy of Social Science*. Cambridge: Cambridge University Press, 1994.

Little, D., *Varieties of Social Explanation*. Boulder, CO: Westview, 1991.

Martin, M., and MacIntyre, L. C., eds., *Readings in the Philosophy of Social Science*. Cambridge, MA: MIT Press, 1994.

Outhwaite, W., *New Philosophies of Social Science: Realism, Hermeneutics, and Critical Theory*. New York: St. Martin's, 1987.

Polkinghorne, D., *Methodology for the Human Sciences*. Albany: SUNY Press, 1983.

Root, M., *Philosophy of Social Science*. Oxford: Basil Blackwell, 1993.

Taylor, C., *Philosophical Papers, Vols. 1 and 2*. Cambridge: Cambridge University Press, 1985.

Postmodern Theory/Poststructuralism

Bernstein, R. J., *The New Constellation: The Ethical-Political Horizons of Modernity/Postmodernity*. Cambridge, MA: MIT Press, 1991.
Best, S., and Kellner, D., *Postmodern Theory*. New York: Guilford, 1991.
Dickens, D. R., and Fontana, A., eds., *Postmodernism and Social Theory*. New York: Guilford, 1994.
Dreyfus, H. L., and Rabinow, P., *Michel Foucault: Beyond Structuralism and Hermeneutics*. Chicago: University of Chicago Press, 1982.
Harvey, D., *The Condition of Postmodernity*. Oxford: Basil Blackwell, 1989.
Lyotard, J.-F., *The Postmodern Condition*. Minneapolis: University of Minnesota Press, 1984.
Madison, G., *The Hermeneutics of Postmodernity*. Bloomington: Indiana University Press, 1988.
Rabinow, P., ed., *The Foucault Reader*. New York: Pantheon, 1984.
Rosenau, P., *Postmodernism and the Social Sciences*. Princeton, NJ: Princeton University Press, 1992.

Pragmatism

Diggins, P., *The Promise of Pragmatism: Modernism and the Crisis of Knowledge and Authority*. Chicago: University of Chicago Press, 1994.
Joas, H., *Pragmatism and Social Theory*. Chicago: University of Chicago Press, 1993.
Thayer, H. S., *Meaning and Action: A Critical History of Pragmatism*, 2nd ed. Indianapolis: Hackett, 1981.
West, C., *The American Evasion of Philosophy: A Genealogy of Pragmatism*. Madison: University of Wisconsin Press, 1989.

Social Constructionism

Gergen, K., *Toward Transformation of Social Knowledge*, 2nd ed. Thousand Oaks, CA: Sage, 1994.
Sarbin, T. R., and Kitsue, J. I., eds., *Constructing the Social*. Thousand Oaks, CA: Sage, 1994.
Shotter, J., *Conversational Realities*. Newbury Park, CA: Sage, 1993.

Symbolic Interactionism

Blumer, H., *Symbolic Interactionism: Perspective and Method*. Englewood Cliffs, NJ: Prentice Hall, 1969.
Denzin, N. K., *Symbolic Interactionism and Cultural Studies*. Oxford: Basil Blackwell, 1992.
Goffman, E., *The Presentation of Self in Everyday Life*. Garden City, NY: Doubleday, 1959.
Joas, H., "Symbolic Interactionism," in A. Giddens and J. Turner, eds., *Social Theory Today*. Stanford, CA: Stanford University Press, 1987.
Plummer, K., *Symbolic Interactionism, Vols. 1 and 2: Classic and Contemporary Perspectives*. Hants, England: Edward Elgar, 1991.

■ About the Author

Thomas A. Schwandt studied English literature and chemistry at the undergraduate level, read systematic theology and process philosophy in seminary, and took his Ph.D. in Inquiry Methodology at Indiana University. For six years he worked as an evaluator in the field of organizational development and training in private industry, then as a faculty member in the Department of Medical Education, College of Medicine at the University of Illinois at Chicago before joining the faculty of the School of Education at Indiana University as Associate Professor. He teaches graduate studies in philosophical foundations of social and educational inquiry, qualitative methodologies, and theory of program evaluation and is a Fellow of the Poynter Center for the Study of Ethics and American Institutions at Indiana University. In recent years he has lectured on qualitative methodology and theory of evaluation in Scandinavia and held a position as visiting researcher at Nordlandsforskning, a sociological research institute in northern Norway. He has authored chapters in *The Handbook of Qualitative Inquiry* (1994), *The Paradigm Dialog* (1990), *Theory and Concepts in Qualitative Research* (1993), *The Quest for Quality* (1994), *Representation and the Text: Reframing the Narrative Voice* (forthcoming in 1997), and coauthored *Linking Auditing and Meta-evaluation* (1989) with E. Halpern; his 30 or so articles on qualitative inquiry and theory of evaluation have appeared in a variety of journals.